R.I.C.H. in Preaching

R.I.C.H. in Preaching

*Transforming Strategic Leaders within an
Afro-Caribbean Congregation to Become Agents
of Radical Inclusive Christian Hospitality
toward the LGBTQ Community through Preaching*

Antonio LaMar Torrence

WIPF & STOCK · Eugene, Oregon

R.I.C.H. IN PREACHING
Transforming Strategic Leaders within an Afro-Caribbean Congregation to Become Agents of Radical Inclusive Christian Hospitality toward the LGBTQ Community through Preaching

Copyright © 2021 Antonio LaMar Torrence. All rights reserved. Except for brief quotations in critical publications or reviews, no part of this book may be reproduced in any manner without prior written permission from the publisher. Write: Permissions, Wipf and Stock Publishers, 199 W. 8th Ave., Suite 3, Eugene, OR 97401.

Wipf & Stock
An Imprint of Wipf and Stock Publishers
199 W. 8th Ave., Suite 3
Eugene, OR 97401

www.wipfandstock.com

PAPERBACK ISBN: 978-1-7252-5254-7
HARDCOVER ISBN: 978-1-7252-5255-4
EBOOK ISBN: 978-1-7252-5256-1

12/18/20

Unless otherwise noted, the Scripture quotation contained herein are from the New Revised Standard Version Bible, copyright @ 1989 National Council of the Churches of Christ in the United States of America. Used by permission. All rights reserved worldwide.

To the invisible congregation of LGBTQ people
who were hurt by the exploitative and exclusionary preaching
within some of the Afro-Caribbean Churches

Contents

List of Table and Charts | ix
Acknowledgments | xi
Abstract | xii
Introduction | xiii

1. RICH Ministry | 1
2. Literature Review | 15
3. Methodology | 35
4. Ministry Implementation, Analysis, and Evaluation | 50
5. Summary, Conclusion, and Reflection | 81

Appendix A: Strategic Planning Initial Assessment Questionnaire | 89
Appendix B: Strategic Planning Participant Feedback Form | 98
Appendix C: Strategic Planning Final Assessment Form | 103
Appendix D: Sermon: A Vision to Rise Up | 106
Appendix E: Sermon: Who Is My Neighbor? | 112
Appendix F: Sermon: Radical, Inclusive, Christian Hospitality in Worship | 118
Appendix G: Sermon: Loving the Stranger in a Culture of Fear | 123
Appendix H: Sermon: Speaking Words of Hospitality | 129
Appendix I: Sermon: Hospitality through Equality and Equity | 136
Appendix J: RICH One-on-One Interviews | 143
Bibliography | 151

List of Table and Charts

Figure 1. Assessment Results of Affinity Circles | 53
Figure 2. Assessment Results of Inviting Others | 54
Figure 3. Assessment of Ideal Equality at TBC | 55
Figure 4. Assessment of Actual Perception of Equality at TBC | 56
Figure 5. Table Assessment for Inclusion at TBC | 57
Figure 6. Questionnaire Results for Sermon One | 60
Figure 7. Questionnaire Results for Sermon Two | 62
Figure 8. Questionnaire Results for Sermon Three | 64
Figure 9. Questionnaire Results for Sermon Four | 66
Figure 10. Questionnaire Results from Sermon Five | 68
Figure 11. Questionnaire Results for Sermon Six | 73
Figure 12. Initial Assessment of Diversity and Inclusion | 77
Figure 13. Results from Final Assessment Questionnaire | 79

Acknowledgments

THE OPPORTUNITY TO ENGAGE and minister as my authentic self has been an invaluable experience. This ministry which began as a research project was made possible by those willing to extend love and hospitality to others. I am grateful to my former congregation, the Cross of Life Lutheran Church in Plainfield, New Jersey, for a mutually rich transformation; to the participants in this ministry from Trinity Baptist Church in Brooklyn, New York; to the covenant group of Dr. Glenmore Bembry, Chris Halverson, Jordan Barbakoff, Dr. Michael Horan, and Dr. Patrick Horan, who reviewed and critiqued various materials; to my advisors and professors, Dr. Carol Patterson and Dr. Lorena Parrish, for planting the idea; to my colleagues at Princeton University, Verita Murrill, and the Diversity and Inclusion Steering Committee for their feedback; to my friends in the New York City Gay Men's Chorus for providing community; and to my mother, Betty E. Jackson, and my husband, James Horan, for their unconditional love.

Abstract

THE BLACK CHURCH IS stereotypically known for its anti-gay and homophobic stance against the lesbian, gay, bisexual, transsexual, and queer (LGBTQ) community. Although statistics have shown a growing amount of support for same-sex couples and gay persons, the patriarchal and heterosexual power structures within the church have been slow to provide welcoming spaces for LGBTQ persons. Furthermore, Afro-Caribbean churches have been reluctant even to address the issue. This ministry measured the responses of the participants within one Afro-Caribbean congregation as they heard transformative sermons about radical, inclusive Christian hospitality (RICH). The ministry sought to inspire them to move from a culture of homophobic hostility toward a community of greater inclusiveness. In doing so, LGBTQ persons would find a safe space for worship and fellowship in the house of God. By using quantitative surveys and qualitative personal interviews, this ministry documented the transformation process of strategic leaders within an Afro-Caribbean church as they heard sermons on RICH.

Introduction

CORNEL WEST ONCE SAID, "Never forget that justice is what love looks like in public."[1] If that is true, then many LGBTQ persons may have never witnessed any justice in the Black Church, though they heard words declaring "I love you" and "We love the sinner but not the sin." But love without justice is just a form of oppression. For many in the LGBTQ community, love was clearly displayed by the former president of the United States Barack Obama, in an interview, where he stated, "At a certain point, I've just concluded that for me personally, it is important for me to go ahead and affirm that I think same-sex couples should be able to get married."[2] It was the first time that a sitting president affirmed the LGBTQ community and its efforts for equality. Yet, many in the Black Church spoke against him and vowed to discontinue their support. For them, President Obama had broken the code of silence regarding the *invisible* population within the Black community and church. He gave LGBTQ persons a voice by advocating for their equality. This former parishioner of a Black liberation preacher, the Reverend Jeremiah Wright, used his presidential status to extend the privilege of liberation to an oppressed group. Jesus once declared:

> The Spirit of the Lord is upon me because he has anointed me to bring good news to the poor. He has sent me to proclaim release to the captives and recovery of sight to the blind, to let the oppressed go free, to proclaim the year of the Lord's favor.[3]

---

1. West, "What Love Looks Like."
2. Gast, "Obama Supports Same-Sex Marriage."
3. Luke 4:17–19 NRSV.

Introduction

The former president knew what others before him (Mahatma Gandhi, Martin Luther King Jr., and Harvey Milk) already advocated: no one is free when others are oppressed.

As many in the United States anticipate the elections for 2020, it seems to be a unique time to be a part of the LGBTQ community. The era since the Supreme Court rulings on marriage equality has seen a complexity of populism of White LGBTQ privilege in mass media. For the first time in its history, the Democratic Party has its first openly gay male candidate, Indiana Mayor Pete Buttigieg, pursuing the presidential nomination. However, in stark contradiction, Black LGBTQ liberation is still bleak. Through it all, it seems that the majority of Black churches remain silent. Since the massacre at the Pulse nightclub in Orlando, Florida, many churches have not advocated for the safety of LGBTQ persons in this country. It may be that some Black churches are afraid that by supporting the LGBTQ victims of hate crimes and violence, they may send a message that they endorse homosexuality. Whatever the reason may be, churches that embrace radical, inclusive Christian hospitality (RICH)[4] recognize that if one group is oppressed, we all are oppressed. As this ministry hopes to serve as a positive example of one church's step toward inclusion, it recognizes that the call to set at liberty those who are oppressed is synonymous with advocacy for those without power and voice.

RICH embraces the concept that "to be radical is to see a vision of the beloved community where justice, peace and love reign."[5] It echoes the Negro Spiritual "You got a right. I got a right. We all got a right to the tree of life."[6] It is a call to liberate the oppressed by extending an invitation to sit at the table with other brothers and sisters and to be included in the kingdom of God. RICH is love in action, establishing a relationship with a diversity of persons, regardless of their race, nationality, gender, gender expression, sexual identity, and orientation. It cannot occur without love. In fact, love without inclusion is neither tokenism nor representation. It is superficial compliance with one's normativity in the social construct of tolerance. In *Radical Love: An Introduction to Queer Theology*, liberationist Patrick Cheng offered an appropriate definition of radical love:

---

4. This is the acronym created by the author and used to describe the ministry entitled "Radical Inclusive Christian Hospitality."
5. Hobbs, "Following the Drum," 19.
6. Pinn, *Terror and Triumph*, 85.

Introduction

> Radical love, I contend, is a love so extreme that it dissolves our existing boundaries, whether they are boundaries that separate us from other people, that separate us from preconceived notions of sexuality and gender identity or separate us from God.[7]

RICH reminds us that nothing can separate us from the love of God. It is childish to think that anything and/or anyone can.

For Black congregations, such as the one used for the context of this research, this ministry sought to use transformational preaching to dissolve the barrier of inauthentic acceptance attached to the "don't ask, don't tell" (DADT) culture within some of the Afro-Caribbean churches. Chapter 1 establishes the foundation for this ministry through a description of the problem of homophobic worship spaces in the Black Church. Using participants of an Afro-Caribbean church as the context for ministry, I offered the purpose of this study, objectives, and definition of terms as related to the ministry.

Chapter 2 provides a description of the biblical, theological, and ministerial issues confronting LGBTQ people of color who are either excluded from the Black Church or exploited for their contributions while complying with its DADT culture. The chapter comprises the literature and resources that informed the sermons and workshops used in RICH.

Chapter 3 discloses the methodology used for RICH in the context of the church chosen for this ministry. It offers the homiletic and hermeneutical methodology for sermons used for the transformation of those participating in RICH. It also documents some of the challenges and adjustments made to the ministry as it grew during implementation.

Chapter 4 documents the implementation, analysis, and evaluation of RICH. In this chapter, the reader will journey with me as RICH is done in the ministerial context. The data from questionnaires, group discussions, and interviews will provide insight into the challenges of one Afro-Caribbean church struggling to liberate itself from a DADT culture.

Chapter 5 offers a summary, conclusion, and reflection of the ministry. As the participants of RICH are transformed, the chapter presents insights into possible next steps for their congregation.

Finally, this ministry is about inclusive liberation. It does not attempt to persuade the reader to employ inclusive hospitality by offering different critical reflections on scriptures that were traditionally used to justify homophobia. It does call the Black Church to continue the legacy of liberation

---

7. Cheng, *Radical Love*, 12.

Introduction

theology by extending the privilege of justice, equality, and love to the LGBTQ persons in their midst and communities. As the Black Church advocates for movements such as Black Lives Matter under a presidential administration that considers Neo-Nazi and White Supremacist groups fine people, it is reminded that queer lives matter, too. Rather than continue to advocate policies of praying the gay away, the Black Church should begin to pray the hate away and embrace loving its neighbors as itself.

1

RICH Ministry

Statement and Analysis of the Problem

THE BLACK CHURCH STANDS at a threshold, one of embracing social justice for the oppressed LGBTQ community or closing its doors in the face of talented and gifted persons seeking a community of faith. As millennials challenge the social constructs of sexuality and spirituality,[1] the Black Church struggles to remain relevant to a generation bringing different values to its pews. While some Black churches are not facing the mass exodus of their millennials, many are still confronted with those who bring a mixture of faith with them when they enter the doors.[2] This ministerial project examines the efforts of one Black congregation to break through traditional cultural taboos and embrace LGBTQ persons through RICH as its strategic leaders hear transformative sermons preached by an openly gay Black preacher. Their mutual journey from a position of skepticism and fear to one of relationship and advocacy should demonstrate the possibility of transforming perceived homophobic congregations into welcoming spaces for all persons. Based upon the spiritual maturation that resulted from my pastorate of an Afro-Caribbean congregation formerly known as the Cross of Life Lutheran Church, I propose that transformational preaching can move similar congregations toward a spirit of radical hospitality that embraces the LGBTQ community.

---

1. Millennials are the demographic cohort with birth years between the 1980s and early 2000s.
2. Parker, "One Size," para. 3.

R.I.C.H. in Preaching

A Personal Journey

As an ordained Baptist minister called to pastor an Evangelical Lutheran congregation bi-vocationally, I knew that this Afro-Caribbean congregation still held traditional views on homosexuality; that is, homosexuality and any variance of it was an abominable sin. As I struggled to reconcile my own sexuality with my spirituality, it was a choice to pastor them under the cloak of heterodoxy, wondering if it would be possible for this suburban Afro-Caribbean church to become a welcoming community to all people, including LGBTQ persons. What would it take for this to occur?

For Cross of Life, it took establishing a relationship of trust, love, and hospitality through transformational preaching. After years of practicing various hermeneutics and homiletics, my preaching still lacked authenticity. There was an invisible wall between the congregation and me that stood for some fourteen years. That wall was a lifelong struggle with my sexual orientation. How could I help shape the identity of this congregation without first acknowledging and embracing my own? After some years of preaching about inclusion and love, my personal transformation led me to come out to my congregation. I discovered that the transformative effects were binary for the church and me. Transformation occurred over time as a result of spiritual growth through constant contact with God's word. Through dialogical learning, the spirit of hospitality that was characteristic of this congregation was extended to me. Although my initial encounter with the Black Church was one of exclusion under negative diatribes against the gay community, this congregation removed that cross of shame and replaced it with the hospitality of acceptance and inclusion. Resultantly, its members stood in witness of the church's first same-sex marriage within its walls—my own. The congregation understood the intent of hospitality as noted in Deuteronomy 10:17–19:

> For the Lord your God is God of gods and Lord of lords, the great God, mighty and awesome, who is not partial and takes no bribe, who executes justice for the orphan and the widow, and who loves the strangers, providing them food and clothing. You shall also love the stranger, for you were strangers in the land of Egypt.[3]

As an Afro-Caribbean congregation comprised of descendants of oppressed and enslaved people, they were reminded of their own liberation

---

3. This and all other scripture references are from the New Revised Standard Version unless otherwise noted.

through the hospitality of compassionate people who sought freedom for all. They welcomed into their midst those who were also being oppressed and marginalized.

There may be other congregations within the Black Church whose members are yearning for inclusive hospitality that embraces the LGBTQ community. Moreover, although society has responded to the call for justice and equality, the majority of Black churches are still resistant to being liberated from its fear and loathing of the queer community. In an interview with Marc Lamont-Hill of *HuffPost Live*, Bishop T. D. Jakes discussed the shifting stance of Black churches on LGBTQ persons and their coexistence: "I think that it's going to be diverse from church to church. Every church has a different opinion on the issue, and every gay person is different."[4] Further, when pressed about his thoughts on LGBTQ persons, he revealed that he has evolved and is evolving. It is a slow progression for the Black Church as it seeks to remain relevant in a changing society.

This hesitancy yields a void in preaching that engages the LGBTQ community. In 2014, the Pew Research Center reported that "a majority of U.S. Christians (54 percent) now say that society should accept homosexuality rather than discourage it."[5] Within this group, 51 percent of historically Black Protestants think that homosexuality should be acceptable.[6] The study demonstrated a growing acceptance of homosexuality among Christian Americans being led by younger generations. As the milieu of congregants and communities becomes more benign toward accepting homosexuality, many pastors and ministers are unprepared to preach transformative sermons that embrace the LGBTQ community. Furthermore, many LGBTQ persons remain withdrawn from churches due to their history of sermonic diatribes against homosexuality. Can the transformation that took place at Cross of Life Lutheran Church be replicated in other churches through preaching? Could a culture rampant with homophobia be transformed to extend inclusive hospitality to others without condemnation and judgment?

---

4. Barksdale, "Bishop T. D. Jakes," para. 3.
5. Murphy, "More U.S. Christians OK with Homosexuality," para. 2.
6. Murphy, "More U.S. Christians OK with Homosexuality," fig. 1.

Description of Context

"Reverend Torrence, I would love to help you with your ministerial project, but would you be comfortable not mentioning your lifestyle and orientation during the process?" It was a question that hit me with a reality check. Although I successfully transformed my former congregation into being inclusive and welcoming, there were still an abundance of Black churches that were not openly welcoming to LGBTQ persons, and especially to openly gay clergy. This question from my mentor, Rev. Dr. Glenmore Bembry Jr., reminded me that although I preached at several White progressive churches as an openly gay man, I had yet to preach at one Black Church since my coming out in 2012. Pastors who were once inviting me to participate in revivals, conferences, and worship services had stopped calling. The stigma of having an openly gay preacher in their pulpits seemed to have created an atmosphere of fear. His question caused me to realize the oppressiveness of my intersectionality. As the pastor of an ELCA congregation,[7] I had the privilege of access to several White liberal churches; however, as an ordained Black Baptist preacher who now professed his gayness, I had no access to the *traditional* Black Church. Could I proceed with the task of moving key leaders of my mentor's leadership team to inclusive hospitality without the pronouncement of my sexuality? I conceded and agreed on the condition that if I were asked, I would tell. I made it clear that I was not ashamed of my sexuality and my marriage.

Yet, it turned out that the concerns of Rev. Bembry about individuals within Trinity Baptist Church (TBC) being homophobic surfaced prior to the beginning of my ministerial project. He had assigned me the task of being the Assistant in Strategic Planning. I made it a point to attend weekly Sunday Worship services six weeks before implementing my project. I even requested *watch care* membership status to demonstrate my commitment to the process of leading them strategically in inclusive hospitality.[8] To introduce me formally to the congregation, Rev. Bembry scheduled me to preach during a Wednesday night revival service. This action was an effort to promote the ministry concerning inclusive hospitality. One week before preaching at the Wednesday revival, Rev. Bembry indicated to me that someone googled me and discovered my same-sex marriage. The person

---

7. Evangelical Lutheran Churches of America.

8. Watch care is a service a Protestant church may provide to watch over individuals who are temporarily unable to attend the church where they hold membership.

made it a point to bring it to the attention of the leaders at their meeting and wanted them to prevent me from preaching because the person did not believe that LGBTQ people should be in positions of leadership within the church. Interestingly, the leaders voted the person down and expressed that they had no issue with me preaching at the church, as well as conducting my research. The issue of LGBTQ people in leadership became a catalyst for the conversation on inclusivity. The decision created space for a contextual ministerial project about TBC's place in the changing neighborhood of the Crown Heights section of Brooklyn, New York.

For ninety-two years, TBC has been a congregation enduring the transition of its community. The church was once a predominantly White congregation. As the congregation changed, the previous leaders gave the title and deed to the American Baptist Churches USA (ABCUSA), who are the official owners of the property, with the understanding that the congregation will always be led by an ABC-ordained minister. Now, it has been declared a historical landmark. The congregation sits under the pastorate of Rev. Bembry. It is predominantly Afro-Caribbean, consisting of 70 percent Caribbean Americans and 30 percent other ethnicities, including Latinos. Regarding gender, it is 60 percent female and 40 percent male. With an average weekly attendance of thirty to forty worshippers, the current worship numbers are a significant decrease from the weekly average of 100 to 125 persons that the church once experienced earlier in the seventeen-year tenure of the current pastor. It has been two years since the congregation has baptized any new converts. Most of the vital few and core leaders are aging. TBC is administratively organized with deacon, deaconess, and trustee boards that oversee several auxiliaries. Despite this, there are a handful of millennials whom the pastor has incorporated into critical decision-making committees. The ministerial staff consists of four ministers from a variety of denominations and experiences. As a Christian Bible-based church, the people are directed to accept the responsibility and mandate of the Lord and Savior Jesus Christ to give clothes, food, and care to those who are in need (Matt 25:35–40). The congregation is very active in outreach ministries and activities with the community. This includes a clothing and feeding ministry, various activities for the seniors, and collaborations with community programs, such as Anchor House (a faith-based intensive residential treatment program) and Begin Again (a program through the Brooklyn District Attorney's office that gives Brooklyn residents the opportunity to deal with summonses for low-level offenses quickly and easily right in their community). In spite of TBC's outreach efforts, the decline in church attendance is inconsistent with their vision statement: *a Christ-directed people, persistently driven by a desire to create disciples and transform lives through the insightful teaching of God's Word.*

TBC remains challenged as its community undergoes gentrification. The church is currently observing the construction of a brand-new apartment building in a once-vacant parking lot next door. Along with this new construction, there is an increase in property values and rents. As of July 2017, Brooklyn had a 5.8 percent increase in its population according to the US Census Bureau. In Crown Heights, central Brooklyn, the population has grown to 292,870 persons. The median age of the current population is 33.41, with 54,860 people being married and 138,982 being single. The ethnic composite consists of 77 percent White, 11 percent Hispanic or Latino, 9 percent African American, 5 percent Asian, and 3 percent other.[9] Among these statistics is the LGBTQ community. New York City contains approximately 756,000 people identifying as LGBTQ,[10] with Brooklyn serving as a home for the largest population.

> Brooklyn is a borough of New York that is well known for its gentrified air of old world authenticity and vibrant community cultural life. Geographically, Brooklyn and neighboring Queens (also very LGBT-friendly) are located on the western tip of Long Island, across the East River from Manhattan. There are more than 2.5 million residents in Brooklyn, which is now also established and often referred to as a separate city. According to our [sic] Gay Realtor Brooklyn, most areas in Brooklyn are completely gay-friendly, with many gay-owned businesses and open displays of affection among same-sex couples.[11]

Yet, according to Gaychurch.org, there are no recorded gay-friendly houses of worship in Crown Heights. Furthermore, in July of 2017, the Anti-Violence Project reported "an anti-gay hate violence attack that occurred in Crown Heights."[12] This is a microcosm of the recorded reports of fifty-two hate violence–related homicides of LGBTQ people in New York City, which is the highest number ever recorded by the National Coalition of Anti-Violence Programs. With these statistics in mind, Rev. Bembry noted

9. US Census Bureau, "Crown Heights."
10. Leonhardt, "New York," para. 2.
11. "Top Gay Neighborhoods," para. 1.
12. Anti-Violence Project, "AVP Learns of an Anti-Gay Incident," para. 1.

that his congregation seems reluctant to embrace LGBTQ persons. He recalled several instances of visiting gay persons to his congregation who, even though they found authenticity in his preaching and in the worship experience, did not feel welcomed by the congregation.

Germane to this, the challenge is reaching the queer community. My own experiences of intersectionality as a gay Black Christian preacher presented challenges of existing in two worlds that are disconnected. Coming out as a gay man to the Christian community was just as challenging as coming out as an ordained minister to the LGBTQ community. For many in the queer community, my role as clergy was viewed contrary to gay liberation and some of its anti-church stances. Furthermore, the church-hurt experienced among many LGBTQ persons is still raw and unresolved. In *LGBT Weekly*, Rev. Dan Koeshall notes:

> Many of us grew up hearing we needed to be saved from sexual sin—especially the "sin" of homosexuality–even going so far as to say AIDS is God's response to gays–and it was the homosexuals that helped cause the devastation of "9/11"! Sin and its feared consequences (some believe it is going to hell) are very real issues for many people today.[13]

For LGBTQ individuals, the relevant questions concern the identity of God and how God blesses their loving relationships as well as their community. Is there a God for those within the LGBTQ tribe? Who is Jesus, and what exactly does it mean for them to call Jesus *Savior*? What does the embodiment of Christ look like for this community that is forsaken and cast out by the church?

Reflecting upon these issues, I acknowledge that there exist cultural and religious views against homosexuality within the Caribbean-American community. Although TBC embraces liberation theology, accepting those who go against their cultural norms is difficult. E. Patrick Johnson points out in his essay "Feeling the Spirit in the Dark" that Black theology declines to envision that the same God who can identify with other oppressed groups—African Americans, Jews, Latinos, and women—can also identify with the LGBTQ community.

---

13. Koeshall, "Nothing Can Separate Us," para. 2.

> We don't have to stop being black to be saved. We don't have to stop being women to be saved. We don't have to stop being poor to be saved. So why should we have to stop being gay and lesbian?[14]

I do not believe that we must negate our sexuality in order to embrace God, nor does God deny our humanity. Thus, it is hoped that ministers using inclusivity in their sermons will help to calm fears and rid homophobia. In addition to using inclusive language, the practitioners must strive to reintroduce the body of Christ to the LGBTQ community. This means acknowledging the hurt perpetrated by the church and the need for reconciliation, healing, and love. For TBC and congregations like it, this transformational preaching ministry hoped to encourage strategic leaders to become the catalyst for inclusive hospitality toward the LGBTQ community.

Purpose of the Ministry

This ministerial project assessed a sermon series that surpasses the traditional hermeneutical models rooted in heteronormativity and incorporates language that is inclusive of the LGBTQ community. The objective of these sermons was to encourage the participants in the RICH training workshops at TBC of Brooklyn, an Afro-Caribbean church, to extend hospitality and to welcome members of the LGBTQ community who are outside of their cultural context. These sermons sought to transform the tribal mindset of former immigrants and ostracized people from perpetuating a culture of oppression and exclusion upon others who do not seem to conform to their traditional values and lifestyles.[15]

Scope of the Ministry

This ministry documented and reported the progress made by the participants of TBC who listened to transformative sermons while attending

---

14. Johnson, "Feeling the Spirit," 108.

15. The word *tribal* is used throughout this project to describe the social cliques and affinity circles that possess strong cultural, ethnic, religious, political, economic, and/or social identity that separate them from others. For this project it is also any group that possess an attitude of "us" versus "them" at any costs which produces a callous disregard for marginalized and disenfranchised persons. This milieu of tribalism can develop a corrupt system of values and ethics which contributes to the humiliation, exploitation, and/or exclusion of LGBTQ persons in the church.

a series of workshops on RICH. Group progress was assessed rather than completing an individual assessment of each of the participants. This was also done to ensure the confidentiality of each participant. This ministry laid down the foundation for the group as it begins to strategically plan the next steps for evangelism and growth amid neighborhood gentrification. As it will be demonstrated, the interest in hearing transformative sermons on inclusion grew beyond the participants of RICH. During the implementation of the ministry, the participants petitioned the pastor for me to preach before the congregation on the subject matter of inclusive Christian hospitality. That action itself demonstrated transformation.

Questions, Objective, and Hypothesis of the Ministry

The premise of this ministry was that there are members within other Afro-Caribbean churches yearning for inclusive hospitality that embraces the LGBTQ community. As congregations wrestle between fundamental interpretations of scripture and practicing an ethos of love toward the queer community, there is a void in inclusive preaching that embraces all persons. As growing percentages of millennials embrace LGBTQ persons, how could aging Black churches continue to exclude a portion of the community? How could Black churches continue to use scriptures to justify this exclusion and not recognize similar actions that were once implemented against their own inclusion? Was it possible to have a theological discussion within the church about the inclusion of LGBTQ persons without dealing with the traditional *clobber passages* and *texts of terror*?[16] Furthermore, could this be done without addressing my sexuality and lifestyle with the hearers?

Thesis Statement

Through preaching about extending hospitality to others outside the cultural boundaries of the ministry context, a congregation holding traditional anti-LGBTQ sentiments may be able to shift its culture to welcome all persons within its walls. Using a sermon series that is reflective of inclusive language and cultural sensitivity, preachers will be able to transform a

---

16. Clobber passages and texts of terror are those verses in the Bible that are commonly used to argue that homosexuality and its lifestyle are a sin.

hostile atmosphere through expounding on themes of hospitality as systematic by-products of diversity, social justice, and equality. Resultantly, the hearers will address the crisis of hostility toward those who may seem like strangers in their midst.

Definition of Terms

For the purpose of this ministry, it is important to explain some terminology used throughout this book.

First and foremost, I used the acronym *LGBTQ* for the lesbian, gay, bisexual, transgender, and queer–identifying community. I do acknowledge that the community is changing and evolving as other identities are bursting forth for recognition, such as intersex, asexual, questioning, and their allies. Since this community is still finding its voice within the liberation movement, for the purpose of this book, I have placed them under the umbrella of LGBTQ; however, I do not want to downplay the importance of the diversity and differences within the LGBTQ community. In addition, I used the words queer and gay throughout the book, recognizing that there is a difference. Although some within the LGBTQ community may find offense with the word queer because of its historical use as an inflammatory slur against the community, for the younger generation, this word appears to be more inclusive and captures the fluidity of identities and sexual expressions found within the community. Contrastingly, gay refers to cisgender males who express same-sex attraction. For the Black Church, it is this particular expression of sexuality that seems to be offensive and a threat to patriarchal power.

Diversity consists of the similarities and differences of identity and life experiences that each of us contributes to a group. Our similarities and differences include race, ethnicity, age, gender identity and expression, sexual orientation, religion, national origin, immigration status, socioeconomic background, and abilities and disabilities, among other social identities and positions. Due to systemic oppression, marginalization may be experienced by people in different ways, and those experiencing intersectional oppression often receive the most negative impacts in society.

Inclusion involves environments that allow people to reach their full potential and contribute their best. RICH attempts to make all people feel valued, welcomed, and affirmed, particularly those who often experience societal marginalization due to their race, ethnicity, age, gender identity and expression, sexual orientation, religion, national origin, immigration status, socioeconomic background, and abilities and disabilities, among other social identities and positions.

Equity is recognizing systemic disparities in how people have access to opportunities and power, particularly in decision-making. Most especially—due to structural, institutional, and interpersonal racism and oppression—people of color, particularly African American people especially of transgender and gender nonconforming experience, are marginalized at higher rates within LGBTQ communities.

Hospitality is the act of creating space for outsiders as they are to become the best that they can be, without the expectation of assimilation or duplication of the host's identity, thoughts, and/or attributes. Value systems may become morphed, but they are enhanced by the gifts and talents of the outsiders to the space that has been created for them.

This ministerial project used the word *traditional* as a description of the conservative views based on the fundamental interpretation of scripture held by the church and some in the Black community against the LGBTQ community. It is also the belief that these interpretations of the Old and New Testaments foster the values that should serve as the moral and behavior code for society. These values include but are not limited to abstinence before marriage, sexual fidelity in marriage, marriage as defined between a male and female, and opposition to homosexuality.

DADT is used as the acronym for the "don't ask, don't tell" practice used in many Black churches concerning the LGBTQ community. It is a custom that allows some LGBTQ people to be active in the church while remaining in the closet and not disclosing their sexuality and/or gender identity to others in the church. Because its participants remain in the closet while contributing to the spiritual life of the church, it is also referred to as the "open-closet" policy.

Millennials are the demographic cohort of the population born between the 1980s and early 2000s. Many of this generation's characteristics may vary by geo-sociopolitical conditions; however, the generation is typically familiar and comfortable with communications, media, and digital technologies, as well as matters of diversity, inclusion, and equity.

Transformational preaching is the process whereby preachers and hearers respond to the illuminated Word of God. It is the communication of God's love as manifested in Christ Jesus that changes hate into love, judgment into mercy, and condemnation into salvation and liberation. In transformational preaching, God gets involved with the hearers, causing a change in their conscience, character, and conduct. It is a dialogical relationship between God and preacher; preacher and hearers; and the hearers and their community.

Limitations

Due to the closure of the original context for ministry in which this project was designed, there were a limited number of preaching opportunities at TBC. To implement this ministry, a strategic planning group was formed by appointing a cross section of key leaders and laity of TBC. Even so, the sessions designed for this group were extended to the overall congregation. With that said, the number of attendees varied per session. The measurement of effectiveness was designed to capture an emotive response toward inclusion within the given period. Additionally, after consultation with the pastor of TBC, there were concerns with preaching sermons that solely focus on the LGBTQ community. He urged me to speak about hospitality in terms of inclusiveness of all diverse cultures. In addition, the request to not voluntarily discuss my sexuality during the workshops would affect the embodiment of queerness during the sermons. This was done to avoid contributing to a hostile reception while being a guest in the pulpit. However, in the final group discussion that was used to evaluate the sermon series, I did share my personal journey to evoke a more in-depth discussion. This was done with the approval of the pastor. That disclosure and discussion were necessary because of the group's desire to continue the ministerial project and formally receive me into its congregation. The process for that transformation will be disclosed later in this book.

Delimitations

This project only sought to "plant the seed" of radical, inclusive hospitality among its participants. In the greater scheme of church growth and inclusion, evangelism and cross-cultural discipleship should follow. In addition, the challenge of this project was to preach in a way that the hearers would be evoked to consider LGBTQ persons as their neighbors in a broader context of inclusivity. Therefore, the sermons preached did not deal with the traditional *texts of terror* that are used as diatribes against LGBTQ persons. The goal was not to argue against their understanding of those passages.

Instead, the scriptures used dealt with love, humanity, and hospitality in general to improve their receptivity of LGBTQ persons. The questionnaires and interviews were designed to measure TBC's willingness to open its doors to LGBTQ persons.

Assumptions

This ministerial project initially assumed that the pastor's description of the congregation as one that was hostile toward the LGBTQ community was accurate and not falsely placed on a culture of people that are typically stereotyped as homophobic and anti-LGBTQ. This project functioned under the assumption that a sermon series on hospitality toward a congregation steeped in the traditional beliefs against homosexuality would be enough to move the hearts and minds of the hearers toward a more inclusive attitude. Furthermore, this project assumed that LGBTQ persons desired to be a part of a loving Christian community.

Significance of the Ministry

While compiling the initial ministry proposal, I recalled a recent incident in the library of a local seminary. While I gathered research materials, a young student worker sought to assist me in pulling my books from the library stacks. He inquired about my role and experience as a pastor. As he began pulling the various books that all dealt with queer theology, he looked at me puzzlingly and asked about my research. I explained to him that the project was about transforming a conservative Afro-Caribbean congregation into an inclusive church that would extend its hospitality to the LGBTQ community. He smiled and whispered to me, "I was asking because I'm gay, but no one here knows." I responded to him that it took me some twenty years to get to a place of confidence and not be afraid to show and share my identity. I added that I hoped the same for him. He stared at me intently and declared, "You are inspiring." That spontaneous exchange embodied the anticipated contribution that this ministerial project should make to the LGBTQ community, the Black Church, and the academy. As many LGBTQ voices are slowly being added to queer liberation theology, there still is a void whereby the Black gay cisgender male has yet to be heard. Horace Griffith, in *Their Own Receive Them Not: African American Lesbians and Gays in Black Churches*, echoes this sentiment regarding the lack of presence of the Black gay voice in Black liberation theology. Homosexuality in the Black community has been a taboo topic. Yet, I too feel that it is equally important to give "voice to a group frequently ignored, denied, dismissed, and rejected."[17] While it is acceptable for LGBTQs to serve as musicians, chorus/choir members and directors, ushers, and other church roles considered low-hanging fruit, these Christian believers have been considered the white elephants in the sanctuaries. They are invisible and do not receive the hospitality of welcome and inclusion. This omission within the Black Church is summarized best by the late James H. Cone when he noted,

> No theological issue is more potentially controversial in the Black Church and community than sexuality. Preachers and theologians tend to ignore it, apparently hoping homosexuals will go away or remain in the closet.[18]

With more and more millennials leaving the church due to a lack of relevance, diversity, and inclusion, staying in the closet and exclusion are no longer options. This ministerial project sought to give local Afro-Caribbean congregations a model and motivation to use radical hospitality toward reconciliation with LGBTQ persons.

---

17. Griffin, *Their Own Receive Them Not*, viii.
18. Cone and Wilmore, *Black Theology*, 2.

2
―――

Literature Review

Literature on Liberation Theology

TRANSFORMATION OF THE HEART, mind, and soul of the Afro-Caribbean Church must begin with a theological discussion of its perspective on homosexuality and its responsibility to their LGBTQ neighbors. This is a discussion whereby the church must return to its love ethic, as it once did during its pursuit of racial equality. Dr. Martin Luther King Jr. described this love as understanding good will toward one's neighbor. He described this type of love as agape:

> It means understanding, redeeming good will for all men, an overflowing love which seeks nothing in return. It is the love of God working in the lives of men. When we love on the agape level, we love men not because we like them, not because their attitudes and ways appeal to us, but because God loves them.[1]

The writer of 1 John 4:8 made it clear that whoever does not love does not know God, for God is love.[2] Jesus modeled that love for his followers and commanded them to do the same, saying, "This is my commandment, that you love one another as I have loved you."[3] The writer of 1 Corinthians 13 described to us the attributes of love:

---

1. King, *Testament of Hope*, 8.
2. 1 John 4:8.
3. John 15:12.

> Love is patient; love is kind; love is not envious or boastful or arrogant or rude. It does not insist on its own way; it is not irritable or resentful; it does not rejoice in wrongdoing but rejoices in the truth. It bears all things, believes all things, hopes all things, endures all things. Love never ends.[4]

This was the principle of love that some of the Black churches, aligned with the Civil Rights Movement, once disseminated as they advocated for social change through racial equality. For its leaders, such as Dr. King, love would be the only power strong enough to move complacent White Christians to extend justice and equality to their neighbors of African descent.

> Love is the only force capable of transforming an enemy into a friend. We never get rid of an enemy by meeting hate with hate; we get rid of an enemy by getting rid of enmity. By its very nature, love creates and builds up. Love transforms with redemptive power.[5]

It is this same love that is now needed to transform the Black Church into a welcoming space for LGBTQ persons as they continue to seek protection from discrimination because of their sexual orientation and identity. Rather than justify the exclusion of the queer community through fundamental biblical interpretations, the Black Church must reconnect with its mission of liberating the oppressed through the power of God's love.

In his book *The Divided Mind of the Black Church*, Raphael G. Warnock discusses the historical struggle within the Black Church between piety and liberation as it still attempts to define its mission. With the emergence of Black theology, the church seems to be in crisis with the development of a complex dilemma and double consciousness of faith that is both evangelical and radical. For a large number of African Americans who are self-conscious and self-identify as "Bible-believing" evangelicals, there is an appeal to authoritative truth claims and a biblical worldview that transcends history, race, and culture.[6] According to Warnock, these claims seem to undermine the Black Church's distinctive legacy and peculiar vocation as the conscience of the American Church, especially when it comes to speaking prophetically for social justice for the oppressed and leading the church into overlooking the problems of sexism and homophobia within its own ranks.

---

4. 1 Cor 13:4–8a.
5. King, *Gift of Love*, 48.
6. Warnock, *Divided Mind*, 140.

> With the encroachment of conservative biblical fundamentalism and its authoritative claims to absolute biblical truth, the black church needs, now more than ever, a critical theological principle for probing the meaning of black Christian identity. It especially needs such a principle as a critical lens in a so-called postracial era in which previous forms of black marginalization morph into new, complex, and intractable systems of social death that are in many ways worse than anything a previous generation of civil rights warriors could have imagined. Moreover, internally the black church needs a sophisticated ethic of accountability that calls the church to examine the contemporary implications of its highest theological and moral claims about itself for those who are marginalized within its own family.[7]

Warnock is correct in concluding that the conversation about questions of inclusion around gender and sexual orientation must go beyond the simplistic appeals to biblical quotations. We must remember that it was similar appeals to scripture that led slavery apologists to stand against the abolitionists' urgent call for liberation.

> The classic protestant assertion, *sola scriptura* never solved a political problem or negated the need to wrestle and work through the communal and continuing dance of hermeneutical assessment, theological engagement, and ethical discernment.[8]

It was instead the African American Christian experiences of a conversation with scripture that produced counterculture piety and critical understanding of the gospel's call to liberation. The Black Church is being called back to a love ethic that supersedes the biblical fundamentalism that once advocated slavery and segregation, whereby it loves its neighbor as itself; a love that is patient, kind, and advocates for the liberation of the oppressed.

For a congregation such as TBC, this author believes that love is the liberating force that will transform the Afro-Caribbean community's demonization of gays. The transformation of the Afro-Caribbean attitude from a hostile tribal mentality toward LGBTQ persons to one of hospitality is in itself liberation. It is a liberation from the oppressive gaze of Black sexuality and its stigmas and liberation from the sin of oppressing *the other*. TBC is being liberated to love and grow in grace. The immaturity of the Black Church in its reluctance to embrace a love ethic that supersedes

---

7. Warnock, *Divided Mind*, 142.
8. Warnock, *Divided Mind*, 143.

sexual expression and orientation can be a form of sin itself. In fact, the comprehension of sin and grace by many in the Black Church needs to shift from one of crime and punishment to one of a Christ-centered model. In the book, *From Sin to Amazing Grace: Discovering the Queer Christ*, theologian Patrick S. Cheng argues the need to move from a crime-based model to a Christ-centered model of sin and grace. Rather than viewing sin and its consequences as crime and punishment, Cheng proffers viewing sin as immaturity or incomplete growth. To mature in Christ is to grow toward grace. He states, "We mess up because we are human beings who have not yet arrived at our final state of maturity."[9] Maturing in Christ is to grow toward grace. It is in this spirit that African Americans have historically been able to conquer the sin of segregation through the principles of civil disobedience, advocating peaceful, nonviolent protest based on a love ethic. Their maturity in grace surpassed the immaturity of inequality and segregation.

Somehow, that maturity has left many Black churches and been replaced with principles of legalism and fundamentalism. They have used the *perceived* sinful crime of homosexuality as a means to label the sexuality of the LGBTQ community as perverse, obscene, and abominable. If, according to James Cone, "racism is America's original sin,"[10] then I would reason that homophobia is undoubtedly the Black Church's original sin. Although the Black Church acknowledges the sexual needs of heterosexual persons through a variety of marriage enrichment programs and heterosexual single ministries that encourage marriage, it fails to express concerns for those who do not comply with the heteronormative paradigm. Cheng notes that

> sin may not only be defined as that which opposes God's revelation in Jesus Christ but as exploitation involving the lack of concern for the needs and desires of another person be it sexual or otherwise.[11]

Grace, consequently, is mutuality in a deep relationship with another person. "It is an awareness and honoring of the well-being of the other, sexually or otherwise."[12] Loving our neighbors as ourselves is the epitome of grace as commanded by Christ. Therefore, as the writer of 1 Corinthians 13

---

9. Cheng, *From Sin to Amazing Grace*, 201.
10. Cone, "Theology's Great Sin," 141.
11. Cheng, *From Sin to Amazing Grace*, 74.
12. Cheng, *From Sin to Amazing Grace*, 75.

emphasized, it is time for the Black Church to "put away childish things" and grow up.

John McNeil, one of the forerunners of Gay liberation theology, sounded the shofar years ago by highlighting that the supreme gift of God is love. In his book *Taking a Chance on God*, McNeil says, "To experience genuine human love, to be part of a community of love is to experience the presence of God."[13] For LGBTQ persons who have been exiled from religious communities and/or families, the longing for community is strong. A church matured in God's grace is called to be that community. The Christian community does not exist for itself, but it is the "battleground of movement from captivity to renewal, from conformity to transformation."[14] Resultantly, the church will continue to face pain and conflict as it wrestles with the false values around it and within it.

For TBC, some of these values rest in the Afro-Caribbean culture of the demonization of gays. Studies such as "Religiosity and Attitudes towards Homosexuals in a Caribbean Environment" demonstrate that in a multireligious environment, the highly religious Caribbean participants were most apt to be intolerant of homosexuality. There appears to be a correlation between intrinsic religious orientation and the exhibition of negative attitudes toward homosexuality. The results of this study "underscore some of the cultural issues that make the Caribbean an especially homophobic society."[15] Considering the ethnic makeup of TBC, this datum is relevant. Currently, there are still nine Caribbean countries with laws criminalizing same-sex acts between consenting adults. These are Antigua and Barbuda, Barbados, Dominica, Grenada, Guyana, Jamaica, Saint Kitts and Nevis, St. Lucia, and Saint Vincent and the Grenadines. From imprisonment to public assaults, LGBTQ members of these countries have endured humiliating and oppressive punishments. Jamaica is perceived to be the most homophobic, with some of its local Jamaican artists and clergy advocating violence against gay men. The authors of this study, Chadee, Joseph, Peters, Sankar, Nair, and Philip, found a direct correlation between people with intrinsic religious orientations and their negative attitudes toward the LGBTQ community. They studied 204 undergraduate students at the University of the West Indies in St. Augustine, Trinidad. Their findings illustrated three things:

13. McNeill, *Taking a Chance on God*, 8.
14. McNeill, *Taking a Chance on God*, 188.
15. Chadee et al., "Religiosity," 21.

1. Religiosity is an essential underlying dynamic in group prejudice.
2. The idea of religiosity goes far beyond the presence or absence of a strong religious affiliation.
3. The manner in which religion is exemplified in a person's life affects one's attitudes toward homosexual practices.[16]

Respondents seemed to be unable to distinguish between the non-accepted behavior and the person. The sinner becomes the sin. I contend that this is compounded by the historical factors of homosexual and incestuous practices used during chattel slavery to oppress and dehumanize Afro-Caribbean slaves: from the fancy maids who were trained for the sexual exploits of their masters to the breeding farms where sons and fathers were made to impregnate their mothers, sisters, and daughters to the *buck breaking practices* where taskmasters disciplined and instilled fear into their slaves by publicly raping the men in front of their children. The biblical sin is also a cultural sin whereby the feminization and domestication of African men are viewed as a continual attempt to oppress Black men and cripple Black families. Theologian Horace Griffin highlights how colonialism and racism used Black sexuality as a weapon to enslave and oppress Africans.

> Negative associations about Black sexuality are familiar to both Anglo and African Americans. Since the Atlantic slave trade and the post-enlightenment's racial classification of humans, Europeans have identified the sexuality of African peoples as debased, immoral, perverse and generally grotesque. European Americans wielded their power to brand Black sexuality as everything having to do with badness: African peoples were understood to be oversexed, to have animalistic large genitals and to be characterized by predatory sexual behavior.[17]

Furthermore, the sexuality of African slaves became a commodity. Professors Mireille Miller-Young and Herbert Samuels of the University of California, Santa Barbara, talks about the link between slavery and its sexual economics:

> Slavery existed as a sexual economy, and black bodies have always been both breeders and concubines. They have been

---

16. Chadee et al., "Religiosity," 21.
17. Griffin, *Loving the Body*, 133.

Literature Review

erotic—kind of illicit erotic commodities in an economy that is built upon our labor.[18]

Since this gaze has been placed on persons of color, efforts have been made within the Black community to adopt conservative sexual mores in order to gain a path to acceptability and respectability in White society. There has been a culture of dissemblance whereby Black communities, more specifically the Black Church, have attempted to dis-identify themselves with sexuality in order to protect themselves from the stereotypes of being hypersexual animals. Therefore, it is no wonder that, for people of color, the classification of LGBTQ persons as contrary to the norm becomes an instrument of power in which, more notably, the Black Church oppresses gay people. Those once oppressed are now misusing their power to oppress a particular class of people—namely the LGBTQ community. Professor Sana Loue of Case Western Reserve University writes:

> The characterization of homosexuality and homosexuals as deviant or sinful by some African American churches may represent an attempt of those who are relatively disempowered within the larger society to retain their power and/or to achieve greater power. In theory, the specification of a clear behavioral boundary between those who have sexual relations with members of the same sex and those who do not facilitate the demarcation between those who are "normal" and those who are "deviant."[19]

That which is perceived as deviant sexuality is an instrument of the once disenfranchised class to elevate themselves above those who do not fit the pattern of acceptable citizens of society. Just as White European Americans used their power to brand Black sexuality as having to do with badness, so the Black Church is using the power of its social piety to brand members of the LGBTQ community as aberrant. This is because many persons of color still believe the path to full citizenship and acceptance in White America requires the full adoption of heteronormativity among other qualities of the prevailing power structure. Thaddeus Russell notes this in his article for the *American Quarterly* whereby he says:

> Leaders of the African American and gay and lesbian civil rights movements have insisted that nonheteronormative behaviors such as sexual promiscuity, the celebration of the self, the embrace of

18. Samuels and Miller-Young, "Sex Stereotypes."
19. Loue, *Understanding Theology and Homosexuality*, 79.

pleasure, and the avoidance of obligation—behaviors historically associated with both African Americans and homosexuals—will block the path to citizenship.[20]

LGBTQ members within the Black community are seen as part of the problem of the gaze laid upon Black America. Therefore, the challenge is to not only disassociate the act of homosexuality from the notion of biblical sin but to disassociate it from the sexual violation and oppression of slavery. A sophisticated theology of Black gay liberation is needed to circumvent the chains of psychological oppression, self-hate, and sexual sterility that still hold the Black Church captive.

Literature on the Non-Inclusive LGBTQ Experience in the Church

In addition to Cheng, I utilized other queer resources such as *Que(e)rying Religion: A Critical Anthology* to develop transformative messages toward improving the welcoming ethos of TBC. In this compilation of essays, contributors offer insights on queer history, tradition, culture, society, scripture, and myths—all of which argue for a connection between religion and sexuality. "They also argue against religious bodies, leaders, and adherents who reject lesbians and gay men as categorically unreligious."[21] Their criticism of the ecclesia is warranted by further studies, such as those done by Sandra L. Barnes. In her journal article entitled "To Welcome or Affirm: Black Clergy Views About Homosexuality, Inclusivity, and Church Leadership," Barnes examines the perspectives among a sample group of Black clergypersons concerning creating welcoming spaces for gays. Her research confirms that, although the majority support such an endeavor, many are still uncomfortable with affirming LGBTQ persons and including them in positions of power in the church. This creates an oppressed population within the church that is seen but not heard. She reveals:

> In these instances, church culture creates contingency spaces where a "don't ask, don't tell" philosophy appears to be the norm. And despite churches that espouse a "whosoever will let him

---

20. Russell, "Color of Discipline," 101.
21. Comstock and Henking, *Que(e)rying Religion*, 11.

come" stance, gatekeepers exist and is [sic]particularly evident for top leadership posts.²²

Considering the influence of the Black pulpit upon its laity, the decision of inclusive hospitality within the congregation rests in the cradle of the language of preachers. Barnes's research further reveals the non-scriptural influences upon these preachers that determine their willingness or lack thereof to welcome LGBTQ persons. Many of these influences deal with the cultural climate of their congregations and their patriarchal, heterosexually-based executive boards. This ministerial project would reveal that TBC fell into this category of "don't ask, don't tell" (DADT), which produced a church narrative of inhospitality and shame.

The invisibility of LGBTQ persons echoes the concerns of intersectionality and further alienates them, harming their health and well-being. Sacred spaces should offer peace and solace for the disadvantaged. Yet the continual negative attitudes can promote stress, as discussed by Michael Mink, Lisa Lindley, and Ali Weinstein in their article "Stress, Stigma, and Sexual Minority Status: The Intersectional Ecology Model of LGBTQ Health." A culture of heteronormativity creates hostile environments for LGBTQ persons and produces the social phenomenon of stigma for members of the group. This culture places a pervasive and continuous strain on LGBTQ people that negatively impacts their health. Moreover, there is an effect on their spiritual health, which is the result of spiritual violence from religious institutions.

> Spiritual violence against LGBTQ individuals can take any number of different forms, ranging from condemnation to casting people out of the church, and can be extremely harmful to LGBTQ individuals' physical, mental, and social health.²³

The continual perpetuation of oppressive behavior is further highlighted in Robert Miller's article "Legacy Denied: African American Gay Men, AIDS, and the Black Church." Miller offers research that explores the religious development and spiritual formation of Black gay men living with AIDS. Through personal interviews, the participants discussed their sense of diminished religious identity due to being ostracized by Christian communities in which they came of age.

---

22. Barnes, "To Welcome or Affirm," 1426.
23. Mink et al., "Stress, Stigma, and Sexual Minority Status," 512.

R.I.C.H. in Preaching

Several writers in the collection *The Greatest Taboo: Homosexuality in Black Communities* lend their voices to echo into the chasm of the vacancy in academia concerning the exile of LGBTQ persons in the Black community. Among them are E. Patrick Johnson and Horace Griffin. Johnson, in his essay, "Feeling the Spirit in the Dark: Expanding Notions of the Sacred in the African American Gay Community," discloses the urge of Black gays to be closer to God and express their sexuality. Shunned from doing so in the Black Church, LGBTQ persons of color find this freedom in the safe spaces of dance halls and nightclubs. Safe spaces within these secular entities afford the LGBTQ person the liberation of expression that the church often prohibits. Furthermore, Black members of the LGBTQ community have been cut off from the advocacy of social justice found in the Black Church and its surrounding communities. This distancing of homosexuality from the African American experience has created a void in Black liberation and justice for members of the LGBTQ community. In his writings, Horace Griffin points out the failure of Black pastoral leaders to address the needs of the Black gay members of their communities. Griffin proffers this notion in both his essay entitled "Their Own Received Them Not," as well as his book under the same title, *Their Own Received Them Not*, wherein he indicates that this failure is due to the perspective that homosexuality is a perversion and sin. This messaging continues the perpetuation of hostility toward LGBTQ persons within their own Black families and churches.

> Many heterosexual family members have estranged and disowned responsible and caring lesbian and gay family members simply because they consider them perverse and sinful individuals in need of change. Within Black congregations, many lives are damaged because of homophobia. African American lesbians and gays, like our heterosexual counterparts, simply seek the freedom to establish and maintain our own sexual relationships and families without the burden of heterosexual harassment, ridicule, and restriction.[24]

Griffin examines throughout his book the unhealthy hostile environment of the Black Church concerning LGBTQ communities. He exposes the culture of deception, denial, and silence.

Griffin urges that the cry for justice be extended to the queer community as liberation models teach us. Not doing so will leave many LGBTQ persons unfulfilled and in search of establishing safe and sacred spaces of their own.

---

24. Griffin, *Their Own Receive Them Not*, 120.

Literature Review

> These common experiences of African American gays lead many to find refuge in those Black communities that do not consider their sexual difference as a problem or antithetical to the inclusive gospel of Jesus.[25]

His book speaks to the cultural dynamics of the African LGBTQ community that the Black Church should reach with hospitality.

Despite the hostile environment of the Christian Church toward gay persons, there still seems to be a hunger for inclusion among LGBTQ persons who struggle with the dual identities of gayness and Christianity. This intersectionality is addressed in Eric M. Rodriguez's study entitled "At the Intersection of Church and Gay: A Review of the Psychological Research on Gay and Lesbian Christians." His research attempts to resolve the question of why LGBTQ persons try to have connections with religious institutions that reject them. In spite of the generalized lack of inclusive hospitality from Christian institutions, "a strong Christian religious faith, and a strong desire to be 'out' as a gay man or lesbian, leads many individuals to try to find some way of dealing with both identities."[26] His findings have indicated that some gay Christians have created "safe spaces where they can practice a version of Christianity that neither condemns nor simply tolerates homosexuality, but instead embraces homosexuals as having been created in God's image."[27] Related to this idea is the paper by Terrill J. A. Winder at UCLA that analyzes the coping mechanisms of young Black gay persons exposed to religious teachings about sexuality within their communities. This author examines how young LGBTQ persons were able to find alternatives to the church, whereby they still could express their spirituality and be affirmed. These alternative organizations have established a message and space of hospitality for young gay millennials. They have tapped into the fact that millennials seek inclusion and diversity in their institutions. If churches such as TBC hope to connect with this generation, they must change their narrative from hostility to hospitality toward the LGBTQ community.

---

25. Griffin, *Their Own Receive Them Not*, 184.
26. Rodriguez, "At the Intersection," 7.
27. Rodriguez, "At the Intersection," 7.

Literature on Inclusive Hermeneutics and Homiletics

The change in the narrative begins with a self-exegesis of the preacher. There is a necessity for all preachers to exegete their unconscious biases in understanding Christology, eschatology, and even cosmology to identify vestiges of diatribes from religious fundamentalism working against liberation. Unless there is a transformative moment in the preacher's consciousness whereby he or she laments the loss of privilege and acknowledges his/her role in the continual narrative of oppression, then the embodiment of the sermon will be forfeited. Authors Emily Askew, O. Wesley Allen, and David Buttrick offer some strategies to preachers who feel led to speak prophetically on LGBTQ inclusion but still need to be pastoral to those in the pews who may disagree. In their book, *Beyond Heterosexism in the Pulpit*, the authors challenge both gay and straight preachers to use inclusive ethical language as they examine homiletical strategies to address the issues of prejudice and discrimination against the LGBTQ community. Although some pulpiteers would not categorize themselves as homophobic, they may still practice forms of sexual prejudices that contribute to personal, institutional, and societal discrimination of LGBTQ persons. The authors conclude that "while we progressive preachers certainly reject such overt oppression of homosexuals, we may unintentionally continue to legitimate heteronormativity and heterosexism (and even homophobia) by the ways we discuss sin in the pulpit."[28] Preachers should conduct a self-exegesis to identify their own biased attitudes as they try to address those that are in the pews.

In *The Liberating Pulpit*, authors Justo and Catherine Gonzalez encourage self-awareness in the process of sermonizing to address the ills of society, noting that

> if we can become aware of the social, political, and economic systems that control our lives, we may then find ourselves on the same side of the struggle as those who are the outcasts of those systems. We can then speak from our own experience of bondage and of the problems and frustrations in seeking to be free. We can know what it means to come to consciousness about our own exploitation, even though we fully recognize that our bondage has been quite comfortable. Only then can we really seek to be free.[29]

---

28. Askew et al., *Beyond Heterosexism in the Pulpit*, 25.
29. Gonzalez and Gonzalez, *Liberating Pulpit*, 28.

Literature Review

The call to inclusive preaching is to recognize the need for a liberating gospel in one's life, to discover in what ways one is oppressed, and to learn about how the same system that oppresses others also oppresses the seemingly powerful. The task for preachers is to reflect upon their captivity and need for self-liberation as well as that of their hearers. It is also the reality that only the gospel can liberate. As preachers, we are only messengers. Justo Gonzalez captures this deconstruction of hubris as follows:

> We believe that we can "do" something about everything. If something does not happen, it is our fault. We can fix it. And it certainly is true that, as Christians, we must do all we can in order to "fix" that which must be corrected. Yet, it is also true that most of us are less powerful and less free than we think we are. One of our constitutive myths is precisely that we are free, that we have the power to change, not only ourselves but also society around us. To discover that we too are oppressed, that our freedom too is curtailed by structures which dominate and even oppress us would be shattering to most of us. Yet, until we make that discovery, we cannot begin to be really free, and to join the struggle for the radical liberation, not only of ourselves, but of the whole of God's creation.[30]

That liberation involves identifying the heteronormative structures that undergird our credos and influence our unconscious biases against LGBTQ persons. These often lead to various forms of microaggressions from the pulpit. Coauthors Cody J. Sanders and Angela Yarber identified several forms of microaggressions in their book, *Microaggressions in Ministry: Confronting the Hidden Violence of Everyday Church*. Defined as brief everyday exchanges that send denigrating messages to certain individuals because of their group membership,[31] microaggressions are prevalent in some sermons and churches, causing emotional injury and alienation. They note that most of these are unintentional.

> While microaggressions are perpetrated every day by a multitude of people, most of us believe that we are generally good human beings who live moral lives and resist the prejudices that beset the society that surrounds us. It is surprising for many of us to learn that we communicate messages that are insulting, invalidating, and subtly denigrating to others based on their racial, gender, or sexual identities. That is because microaggressions, by definition, are perpetrated outside the conscious awareness of perpetrators,

---

30. Gonzalez and Gonzalez, *Liberating Pulpit*, 25.
31. Sanders and Yarber, *Microaggressions in Ministry*, 11.

typically quite unintentionally, and often against the conscious self-perception, we hold about ourselves as good, moral people.³²

In a separate article, "Preaching Messages We Never Intended: LGBTIQ-based Microaggressions in Classroom and Pulpit," Sanders suggests that examination should be given to the subtly aggressive speech acts that are perpetrated against the gay community in the variants of microaggressions, such as microinsults, microinvalidations, and microassaults. Although they may be unintentional due to the internalized heterosexist bias and prejudice against gender variance, microaggressions may creep in our messages and perpetuate stereotypes and degradation of the LGBTQ community. For example, there are often times when those in the pulpit declare, "We need more men in this church." Such a statement invalidates non-cisgender males who are present in the church. Or, ignoring the preferred pronouns of nonbinary gender people may be perceived as a microinvalidation because their identity is continually being invalidated. For the Afro-Caribbean church, these microaggressions may resonate through various forms of tokenism. As LGBTQ persons participate in music ministries, they are often exploited for their musical talents and complimented as the model minority for their communities. As long as they adhere to the DADT cultural norms of the church, they are perceived as normal. This silence sends the coded message that any expression of their lifestyles is abnormal.

The task is to take on a new hermeneutical lens and expose ourselves in interpreting theology differently, whereby we are querying and queering our boundaries and binaries. Carolyn Brown Helsel in "Queering Straight Preaching" challenges preachers in their sermon preparation to address the hermeneutic of misrecognition. They should not approach a sermon just thinking about mechanisms to help make their congregations more welcoming to LGBTQ persons, but rather they should ask difficult questions regarding their interpretation of texts and preaching, such as, "How have I misrecognized my own queerness and the queerness of my congregation? And, how may we be transformed if I took greater risks in preaching about the gifts of others?"³³

The fact is that for many full-time pastors whose income is solely reliant upon their congregations, some of these risks are not taken. They stand to lose much. No other preacher may know this as well as Carlton Pearson does. He tells of his journey from Christian Fundamentalism to Christian

32. Sanders and Yarber, *Microaggressions in Ministry*, 14.
33. Helsel, "Queering," 18.

inclusivity in his book *The Gospel of Inclusion*. Although the book explores elements of the doctrine of universalism, Pearson promotes *inclusion consciousness* as preachers speak on the principles of salvation, faith, and grace. It is a challenge to reimagine God through the perspective of inclusion, and likewise, the traditional interpretation of *imago Dei*. Pearson's perspective on inclusion is appreciated, but I do not feel that a radical shift in doctrine is needed to justify hospitality to LGBTQ persons. Promoting a consciousness of inclusion may transform the Afro-Caribbean community's negative attitude toward gays. There is agreement that transformative preaching involves the lament of loss within the preacher. Pearson reflects on this loss through his experience of losing a six-thousand-member ministry as he began to preach a gospel of inclusion. He declares that

> I will no longer conform to a doctrine that holds so many in blind, unreasoning fear of social and cultural reprisal. That is totalitarianism. Do I miss my old life? You bet I do! No one wants to be an exile on an island of his own making . . . but as Jesus once asked, "what does it profit a man to gain the whole world and forfeit his own soul?"[34]

Proclaiming a gospel of radical, inclusive Christian hospitality involves lamenting a loss of privilege as the preacher seeks to liberate the oppressed from their oppressors—heterosexist churches.

Literature on Inclusive Hospitality

Moving from hostility to hospitality involves Christians creating a poverty of mind; that is, a hunger for digesting and processing the needs of their guests in order to host them better. It is that task that transforms the hosts from hurters to healers. Henri Nouwen's contribution to this philosophy is captured in his book *Reaching Out*. Using his methods of creating free space, whereby guests can be liberated, is the paradigm that this ministry will need to be successful. Niceness, tolerance, and complacency do not translate into welcome. Nouwen stresses the importance of acknowledging our biases, implicit and unconscious, and employing a *poverty* of mind and heart. As hosts, Christians are urged to empty themselves of preconceived ideas, constructs, and stereotypes and create a "friendly space where we can reach out to our fellow human beings and invite them to

---

34. Pearson, *Gospel of Inclusion*, 282.

a new relationship."³⁵ His tri-movement of spiritual hospitality echoes the thoughts of Paulo Freire in *Pedagogy of the Oppressed*. Transformation is a dialogical process. For the ministerial context, those subscribing to a heterosexual binary lifestyle are in authority. Hospitality must be extended in a forum where they do not assume innate superiority, purity, and civility above their guests and bank information into their lives. The process is one of mutual pedagogy for the empowerment of both parties. Freire expounds on this form of discourse as banking:

> We must never merely discourse on the present situation, must never provide the people with programs which have little or nothing to do with their own preoccupations, doubts, hopes, and fears—programs which at times, in fact, increase the fears of the oppressed consciousness. It is not our role to speak to the people about our own view of the world, nor to attempt to impose that view on them, but rather to dialogue with the people about their view and ours. We must realize that their view of the world, manifested variously in their action, reflects their *situation* in the world. Educational and political action which is not critically aware of this situation runs the risk either of "banking" or of preaching in the desert.[36]

Hospitality is dialogical, requiring faith in the best of humanity. Freire writes:

> Dialogue further requires an intense faith in humankind, faith in their power to make and remake, to create and re-create, faith in their vocation to be more fully human (which is not the privilege of an elite, but the birthright of all). Faith in people is an a priori requirement for dialogue; the "dialogical man" believes in others even before he meets them face to face.[37]

The implications of hospitality extend to social advocacy for justice, as well. Radical, inclusive Christian hospitality expands the concept of *diakonia* to include social justice through advocating for the rights, justice, and equality of the oppressed and marginalized.[38] In order to have a hospitable mindset of inclusion, pedagogy must include an acknowledgment that often churches are exclusive in their outreach ministries. Words and actions must declare: "*Dum vivimus servimus*"—while we live, we serve.

35. Nouwen, *Reaching Out*, 71.
36. Freire, *Pedagogy of the Oppressed*, 96.
37. Freire, *Pedagogy of the Oppressed*, 91.
38. Diakonia is the ministry of service to the poor and oppressed.

Then the church can honestly have its hand on the pulse of the community as it strives for inclusion and equity to obtain a dream that can no longer be deferred. Such activity is described by Jayme R. Reaves in the book *Safeguarding the Stranger*. Reaves takes hospitality to the next level by describing *protective hospitality*, as demonstrated in the Abrahamic theology of Judaism, Islam, and Christianity. He defines protective hospitality as "the provision of welcome and sanctuary to the threatened other, often at great risk to oneself."[39] Reaves's research demonstrates some of the historical and contemporary applications of protective hospitality through various communities that provided safe houses and sanctuary for foreigners in defiance of governmental laws and policies, such as the Catholic church hiding Jews during Nazi-occupied Germany and villages aiding refugees from the genocide and ethnic cleansing in Bosnia and Croatia. In the United States, religious communities have participated in the Sanctuary Movements of the 1980s to respond to the needs of those fleeing the violence of Central America. It is a movement that some churches reignited under the current president of the United States' agenda to expel undocumented persons. Reaves analyzed the motives for many of the faith-based communities and discovered that, although many could not theologically articulate the reasons for defying legal and social norms for assisting strangers, there was a priority of hospitality and welcome that surpassed religious, ethnic, or moral purity. Those providing the welcome stood in solidarity with the strangers (the others). For the Black community, which birthed the Black Church, it was the abolitionists and the inhabitants of houses and churches along the Underground Railroad that provided a welcoming place to escaped slaves seeking freedom. As beneficiaries of protective hospitality, the Black Church should pass it on to those who are being ostracized by society. Those who have been liberated should seek to liberate others. There is where the power of hospitality lies. "Protective hospitality's power lies in welcoming or being welcomed by an *other*; protection given by the same is not hospitality but filial or communal obligation."[40] When faith communities make it a priority to welcome others whom society deems as different, then transformation occurs.

---

39. Reaves, *Safeguarding the Stranger*, xii.
40. Reaves, *Safeguarding the Stranger*, loc. 7368.

Literature on the Electronic Pulpit and Sermon Form

Coming from corporate America, I spent decades giving and watching presentations through a variety of technological media. As society has embraced and become engulfed by a culture of screens, be it televisions, smartphones, and tablets, some churches have been slow to respond to the trend. Our society is visual as well as aural. Imaginations are no longer stimulated by descriptive prose and metaphors. Information is processed immediately. In the study "Technology in Spiritual Formation: An Exploratory Study of Computer Mediated Religious Communication," done by Susan Wyche, Gillian Hayes, Lonnie Harvel, and Rebecca Grinter, the researchers concluded, "The use of technology for spiritual formation simultaneously incorporates unique and familiar patterns of interaction."[41] Their study observed churches that varied in size and discovered that for some pastors, there was a different level of expectations with the use of media. Older and smaller churches felt the need to provide some of these services, although some of their congregants were comfortable with a technology-free environment. Yet, many preachers benefited from the iconography and modern photography that use of such software as PowerPoint allowed them to incorporate into their sermonic presentations. The effectiveness of the presentations was dependent upon the preacher's aptitude with technology. Transforming an Afro-Caribbean church to embrace hospitality toward the LGBTQ community will require an envisioning and/or embodiment of the Word. During the Civil Rights Movement, many Christian churches were drawn to advocate for racial equality as they witnessed the televised broadcasts about marchers being beaten with batons, drowned with water hoses, and bitten by police dogs. There is a need for the visual impact of the injustices against the LGBTQ community for those with eyes to see and ears to hear. This may not be as explicit and violent as the images portrayed during the Civil Rights Movement, but they should be prolific.

In *Envisioning the Word*, Richard Jensen advocates that preachers should think in pictures to bridge the communication gap with today's hearers. This ministry utilized the thought process of Jensen by presenting audiovisual sermons that were complemented by words and images to provide a holistic seeing and hearing experience. "Today's churchgoers, steeped in multimedia communications, have been trained to think and

---

41. Wyche et al., "Technology," 207.

learn with their eyes and ears together."[42] Images do not replace words, but they can assist the receiver in accepting the message and grasping the crux of the sermon. "Our teaching and preaching need a new way of integrating words and images."[43] For this evolution in preaching, Jensen offers three basic types of suggested sermon structure for using images: *thinking in idea*, *thinking in story*, and *thinking in image*.

I concur with the *thinking in idea* structure, whereby the core structure of the sermon is the careful arrangement of ideas. Visual images and words are projected in parallel to each of the major points of the sermon. "One might call this a kind of double-track sermon."[44] There is an explanation of the scripture and its ideas, along with projected images that illustrate the point being made. Words are illustrated by images. Images accompany words. This can be a very effective way of getting one's points across.[45]

The goal is to make the point to the audience. A clear organization of sermon moves is recommended. Samuel Proctor, in *The Certain Sound of the Trumpet: Crafting a Sermon of Authority*, declares that "before a sermon goes anywhere, the preacher must have focus and direction."[46] Using Proctor's dialectical approach model assists with structuring the images to the moves of the sermon as it proceeds. These moves are subject, text, introduction (antithesis), transition (thesis), relevant question, and a synthesis consisting of three to four points. These moves help the preacher to organize the imagery being used throughout the sermon.

There are critics who condemn the use of PowerPoint in sermons, referring to it as a fancy version of the slide projector. Philip Quanbeck, in his article "PowerPoint in Preaching? No!" claims that PowerPoint corrupts because it weakens verbal and spatial reasoning.

> The inner workings of PowerPoint want to make you conform to its way of thinking. PowerPoint wants the user, you, to think in bulleted lists, it wants titles for slides, it offers the user an array of colorful, eye-catching, and ultimately distracting backgrounds.[47]

---

42. Jensen, *Envisioning the Word*, 5.
43. Jensen, *Envisioning the Word* 10.
44. Jensen, *Envisioning the Word*, 126.
45. Jensen, *Envisioning the Word*, 126.
46. Proctor, *Certain Sound of the Trumpet*, loc. 322.
47. Quanbeck, "PowerPoint," 422.

I agree with Quanbeck that preaching is about the Word; however, media such as PowerPoint and Keynote are tools whereby the Word can be augmented. The fear that the audience will look past the preacher to the image on the screen and will prefer *looking* rather than *listening* is an egotistically biased fallacy. Preachers often plead that God would hide them behind the cross so that hearers can see the Christ in them as they deliver the Word. Presentation tools give them that opportunity. The effectiveness of the multisensory sermon is significantly affected by the skill of the presenter. The key is not to broadcast blocks of text and bullet points but to push the boundaries of one's creativity and utilize images and video clips as illustrations. Proponents such as Andrew Root give the best advice to preachers using slideware.

> Write your sermon without having the slideware in mind at all. Write it faithful to the text and to the people that will hear it. Then after the sermon is finished, read through it and think about what pictures would enhance and connect with your message—professional, high quality pictures, not lame clip art.[48]

The key to using images throughout one's sermon is not to refer to the images and presentation but allow them to provide background conceptual texture to the message. The image is not the message, but it should draw people more deeply into the sermon to transform them from hostility to hospitality; from exclusion to inclusion; from injustice to equality.

---

48. Root, "PowerPoint," 423.

3

Methodology

THE PREMISE OF THIS ministerial project was that transformational preaching about RICH would shift an Afro-Caribbean congregation from a culture of anti-LGBTQ sentiments to one of inclusive hospitality toward LGBTQ people. To measure the effectiveness of the sermons, I first assessed the participants' attitudes toward inclusivity with a survey. Thereafter, as the workshops proceeded, I used quantitative surveys to measure the hearers' willingness to welcome all persons, including LGBTQ people. These were taken after each sermon was preached. Throughout the implementation of this project, I facilitated group discussions and conducted individual interviews with some of the participants. The interviews and group discussions gave insight into the DADT culture at TBC that could not be determined through the surveys. As this project proceeded and grew in its success, revisions to the survey were made to assess the sermons. This also accommodated the growing interest of the participants in the project.

The Design of the Ministry

This ministry was aimed at transforming a group of key strategic leaders at TBC to become agents of RICH toward members of the LGBTQ community. Identified by the pastor of TBC, the invited participants were to begin thinking strategically about inclusive church growth through evangelism and outreach. Therefore, it would be critical for this group to embrace RICH as a mechanism. They were a composite of deacons, trustees, deaconesses, worship leaders, ministers, and laity. In addition, the original six scheduled workshops would be open to all TBC members. This would cause variances in attendance and made the tracking of individual transformation during the sessions difficult. For TBC, the concern was making sure that all interested members had the opportunity to attend the sessions for the purpose of transformative ministry. Furthermore, TBC was some significant distance from my residence. With the busy holiday calendar of TBC's various ministries and services, it was decided to conduct one session in mid-November, two sessions in December, and the remaining three in January. An alternate date in case of inclement weather was also scheduled. The workshops would occur on Saturday mornings, with two planned for Wednesday nights in place of the church's weekly Bible study.

As the ministry proceeded, the schedule would be adapted to accommodate the demand for more inclusion of the congregation. By the third session in December, the participants wanted more of the congregation to hear a message on RICH. Working with the pastor, I modified the schedule for January to include a Sunday morning sermon. The alternate reserved date would be a group discussion and interview about the sermons and inclusivity.

Therefore, this ministry had to be designed to track the progress of the group as a composite of TBC over the three-month period. The individual transformation would be discussed during interviews and group discussions. In order to measure the transformation of the group toward inclusion, a mixed-method approach of qualitative and quantitative analysis was utilized. Using an Initial Assessment Questionnaire (appendix A), I attempted to capture the participants' attitudes of hospitality to others outside of their cultural norms. This helped to establish a baseline that calculated their diversity and inclusion concerns. Other than requesting basic facts on the participants' genders and ages, the questionnaires were anonymous. In addition, this ministerial project used narrative research for its qualitative aspect through recorded group discussions and interviews with the permission of the participants. Using an Informed Consent Form (appendix B), I assured the participants that their answers and identities were to be kept safe and undisclosed throughout this ministry. During each session, an Informed Consent Form was discussed, documented, and gathered. Throughout the process, attendance was taken in the workshops to track the number of participants and to determine who needed to complete the Informed Consent Forms. Those declining to complete the form were

Methodology

still permitted to attend the workshop sessions, but their verbal comments and feedback were removed from the group interviews. However, participation in the final group discussion and interview required completion of the Informed Consent Form.

During each workshop, a sermon was preached to motivate the hearers to extend hospitality toward others, including the LGBTQ community. After each sermon, the hearers were asked to complete a sermon evaluation questionnaire (Strategic Planning Participant Feedback Form, appendix C) to determine their comprehension of the sermon and their thoughts on RICH. These questionnaires were anonymous, and they measured their responses along the ranges of *Strongly Agree*, *Agree*, *Disagree*, and *Strongly Disagree*. The goal was to determine the transformative effects of the sermons on the group.

At the end of the training in January, a group interview was held and recorded with the consent of the participants. They were shown a summary compilation of their initial responses regarding equality, inclusivity, and hospitality. The areas where there were significant variances became the focal points for discussion. During this session, the participants were also asked to give a verbal assessment of the sermons that they heard. They also completed the Final Assessment Questionnaire (appendix D). This group discussion was conducted due to the unavailability of many of the participants for personal face-to-face interviews. Distance, inclement weather, and schedules made some individual interviews impossible. In addition, it was apparent during the process that many participants were not comfortable with a telephone conversation as well as a video conference. As a newcomer to TBC, I had to build a level of trust. Eventually, there were some participants willing to participate in face-to-face interviews.

Sermon Design and Presentation

Technology and social media have shifted the atmosphere of communication in society. We are a visual and aural community. According to a Nielson Consumer Report in 2016, adults in America were "spending an average of ten hours and thirty-nine minutes each day consuming media, be it through tablets, smartphones, computers, and televisions."[1] PowerPoint and video clips were used to capture the attention of the participants, based on the fact of human visual consumption. In addition, the visual

---

1. Howard, "Americans," para. 2.

images reinforced the point of the message being communicated. Each sermon followed a didactic format as outlined in Samuel Proctor's *The Certain Sound of the Trumpet: Crafting a Sermon of Authority;* that is, it included a "subject, text, introduction (antithesis), transition (thesis), relevant question, and synthesis."[2] With this in mind, the sermons and subject matters of the workshops were designed to prophetically preach about the inclusion of the LGBTQ community in the context of extending hospitality to all persons. The sermons would not attempt to convince the hearers that homosexuality was not a sin but instead encourage them to implement a love ethic of equality and justice for all persons, regardless of sexual identity and orientation. All sermons were approximately twenty to twenty-five minutes in length.

Sermon One—A Vision to Rise Up (Acts 10:34–43)[3]

During the prior month of October, the congregation was called to pray and fast for vision. Confronted with declining attendance and gentrification, the leadership attempted to get the church body prepared for visioning. Since this ministry would start in the following month, an appropriate text seemed to be the story of Peter's vision about being told to slay and eat from a sheet filled with unclean animals, insects, and birds. It is a vision of the Gentiles being welcomed and received into the early church by God. Yet, Peter must confront his prejudices and biases, which are based on his understanding of Mosaic law—specifically, parts of Leviticus, whereby the people are commanded to refrain from consuming creatures deemed unclean. There are other traditions, rituals, and practices considered unclean and/or banned in Leviticus, such as wearing mixed fabrics, piercing body parts, decorating selves with tattoos, and mistreatment of foreigners, as well as menstruation and various expressions of sexuality.

The participants were shown a brief movie clip which reenacted Peter's vision,[4] visiting Cornelius, and concluding that God shows no partiality. It was produced by the Church of Jesus Christ of Latter-day Saints. The theme of the sermon was that to achieve a vision of inclusion, we must confront our personal issues of unconscious and conscious biases. Peter's bias against uncleaned animals was compared with our own beliefs concerning

2. Proctor, *Certain Sound of the Trumpet*, loc. 347.
3. Appendix E.
4. CJCLDS, "Peter's Revelation."

that which is unclean and unacceptable. We all are capable of bias, according to the author and psychologist Claude Steele. In *Whistling Vivaldi: How Stereotypes Affects Us and What We Can Do*, Steele says:

> We simply are not and cannot be, all-knowing and completely objective. Our understandings and views of the world are partial and reflect the circumstances of our particular lives.[5]

Becoming more self-aware does not purge us of bias, but it can help us to understand and constrain it. Peter's desire to fulfill the command of Christ enabled him to question his fundamentalism. The love that was extended to him from Christ compelled him to now extend it to others. Thus, the commands to rise, resist, and receive are applicable to all people who are reluctant to go beyond their comfort zones and extend hospitality to people of different races, cultures, and sexual identities and orientations. The call is to rise above our level of comfort, resist our biases, and receive others through hospitality.

Sermon Two—Who Is My Neighbor? (Luke 10:25–37)[6]

As TBC confronts gentrification, the question "Who is my neighbor?" asked of Jesus by the lawyer in Luke 10:25–37 becomes both real and relevant. The members of TBC face the changing demographics of Crown Heights every time they commute to church. In addition, the construction of a new apartment building next door presents an opportunity to reach out to new persons. After the text was read, the audience was shown a contemporary clip illustrating the parable of the Good Samaritan. It was produced by the Church of Jesus Christ of Latter-day Saints.[7] The victim was portrayed as a white male construction worker leaving a worksite at night in the heart of an urban community. Beaten and robbed by masked assailants, he was left for dead in an alley until morning, when he awakened and crawled to the main street. The pedestrians rushed to avoid him and ignored his pleas for help. Then a young African woman noticed him, went to his aid, brought him to a clinic, and waited with him until he received care. In the meantime, her backstory was shown. She flashed back in her memory to when she was crossing a desert as a refugee seeking assistance. In addition,

---

5. Steele, *Whistling Vivaldi*, 14.
6. Appendix F.
7. CJCLDS, "Good Samaritan."

we learned that while she was aiding this victim, she was late for her first day at work at her new job. This video clip illustrated the text, and it became the springboard for challenging TBC's concept of hospitality to strangers. Once strangers themselves in the United States, many Caribbean audience members should have related to the story of the woman in the clip, not as refugees but as immigrants in a new country. They, too, were once strangers who were dependent upon the hospitality of others.

This sermon defined what it means to move radically beyond one's comfort zone and extend hospitality to strangers. The biblical parable did not tell the hearer the identity of the victim. All that was known is the man fell among thieves. Nothing besides his gender—not his physical identity, economic status, religious affiliation, or moral character—was discussed. For Jesus, that was not important. It was the actions and inactions of those around him that pushed this story forward: the thieves, the priest, the Levite, the Samaritan, and the innkeeper.

The Samaritan took the risks that the avoiders would not: the risk of contamination, the risk of attack, and the risk of financial loss. Jayme Reaves noted that "Jesus' call to protective hospitality illustrates the sacrifice, risks, and unexpected nature of caring for the threatened other."[8] Although others who hold to fundamental interpretations of texts and regard themselves as religious may tend to avoid strangers and their strangeness because of what they interpret from scriptures, Christians were commanded to love. Loving others causes them to radically challenge religious and social norms and offer mercy to others despite their permeating fears—a RICH church practices protective love.

Yet, the story did not end with the act of the Good Samaritan. An assignment was given to the innkeeper to whom the Samaritan brought the victim for care. The innkeeper was told to care for the victim and was promised compensation for his/her expenses upon the return of the Samaritan. The church is responsible for reaching and aiding the helpless through evangelism and missions, as well as continual caring for those assigned to its ministry through pastoral care and discipleship. In order to reach the lost, the church must venture out in a model of evangelism and outreach. This sermon confronted the tribal nature of TBC's evangelism and outreach. That nature was one where the participants tended to reach out to those who are similar to them in identity. The sermon questioned how far they were willing to extend their hospitality to others. Using Ralph Winter's

---

8. Reaves, *Safeguarding the Stranger*, loc. 2518.

Methodology

diagram of the evangelism scale,⁹ this sermon evoked TBC to examine the impact of reaching out to others beyond their affinity circles.

The Good Samaritan did not discriminate against the victim but instead demonstrated mercy. When Jesus asked him, who was a neighbor to the victim, the lawyer responded that it was the one who showed him mercy. Then the edict from Jesus was to go and do likewise. I surmised that the Good Samaritan was not alone in showing mercy but the innkeeper as well who was told to care for the victim on the promise of the Samaritan. Therefore, to imitate the acts of mercy in this story, one's actions must involve approaching the helpless, associating with them, attending to their hurts and needs, assisting them with provisions, and taking the assignment of being a caretaker to them until their recovery. All this activity pivots on RICH.

Sermon Three—RICH in Worship (Revelation 7:9–17)¹⁰

After the scripture was read, a video clip from the archives of *Meet the Press* was shown of Rev. Dr. Martin Luther King declaring that the most segregated hour in America occurs on Sunday morning.¹¹ This was the antithesis of the sermon. Proctor described the antithesis as

> an error that must be corrected, a condition that must be altered, a mood that must be dispelled, a sin that cries out for confession and forgiveness, some ignorance that needs to be illumined, a direction that has to be reversed, an idolatry of worshipping things that are corruptible that should cease in favor of praising an incorruptible God, some pain and hurt that awaits the balm of Gilead, or some lethargy that needs to be replaced.

Bryan Chapell, in *Christ-Centered Preaching: Redeeming the Expository Sermon*, called this transgression as *the fallen condition focus*. This "is the mutual human condition that contemporary believers share with those to or about whom the text was written that requires the grace of the passage for God's people to glorify and enjoy him."¹²

---

9. Winter and Koch, "Finishing the Task," 16.
10. Appendix G.
11. King, "Most Segregated Hour."
12. Chapell, *Christ-Centered Preaching*, 29.

R.I.C.H. in Preaching

The fallen condition of the church is that some sixty years after Martin Luther King's statement, the church is still segregated and exclusive. According to Pew research in 2014, "eight in ten churches were dominated by at least 80 percent of one ethnic group."[13] Yet, church officials, such as Lovett Weems, note that millennials are "more diverse and the church is getting older and less diverse."[14] As "the most ethnically diverse generation in the history of the United States,"[15] millennials expect this diversity duplicated in their institutions. The Rainers, in *The Millennials: Connecting to America's Largest Generation*, echo this sentiment:

> Diversity is commonplace for the Millennials more than any previous generation. It is a nonissue. For Millennials diversity is a matter of fact. It is simply our reality. The friendships made in the Millennial Generation reflect our diverse world. A majority of Millennials claimed at least some friendships with people who are different from them in race, lifestyle, age, and religious beliefs. Millennials have friends who look different, act different, and believe different.[16]

The challenge for TBC in this sermon was to aspire to the vision of John, the Revelator, whereby he described an unmeasurable number of diverse people from every nation worshipping at the throne of God. As they envision for themselves a church filled with the younger generation, the hearers need to realize that a call to an environment of reductionism will not suffice for millennials.

Therefore, the task for the hearers of this sermon is to grasp the God of the church that they go to rather than the church of the God they worship. Worship is inclusive because salvation is inclusive. Salvation is inclusive because Jesus Christ, the Lamb of God, is inclusive. The sovereignty of God to redeem others regardless of race, class, gender, sexual identity, and orientation is beyond the power and scope of the church.

Using excerpts and images from prominent people of African heritage, this sermon helped to shape the vision of diversity in worship for the hearers. These include various perspectives of diversity from Bishop Desmond Tutu, author Audre Lorde, and civil rights activist Coretta Scott King, who continued the legacy of her husband by advocating for those in the LGBTQ

---

13. Lipka, "Many U.S. Congregations," para. 3.
14. Hahn, "Church," para. 4.
15. US Census Bureau, "Millennials," para. 1.
16. Rainer and Rainer, *Millennials*, 52.

community. She appealed to those who believed in Martin Luther King's dream to make room at the table of brotherhood and sisterhood for lesbian and gay people. This is the challenge for many Black churches concerning inclusivity—extending a welcoming embrace to the LGBTQ community.

Sermon Four—Loving the Stranger in a Culture of Fear (Deuteronomy 10:12–19)[17]

Hospitality is God's love made visible. As God loved the Israelites when they were foreigners in the land of Egypt, Moses reminded them to love the foreigner in their midst. This command was also echoed in Leviticus 19:33–34. The hearers of this sermon were reminded to set aside their fears and welcome the stranger in their midst. Despite the dangers that may be involved, hospitality entails the sacrifice of one's safety. This is the risk for people who are empowered to love others as themselves and work for justice. During this sermon, the hearers were reminded of the nine parishioners in Charleston's Emanuel AME church. They were massacred by a young White male whom they invited into their prayer and Bible study meeting.[18] They died displaying a love ethic that Jesus taught. The hearers were also reminded of the lack of hospitality that our society has displayed to others who are perceived as foreigners in our communities: a hooded Trayvon Martin, the caravan of migrant workers and refugees approaching the southwestern border of the United States, or individuals donning Islamic clothing. These incidents have contributed to a culture of xenophobia. In fact, Henri Nouwen noted that "it does not require much social analysis to recognize how many forms of hostility are usually pervaded with fear and anxiety, prevent us from inviting people into our world."[19]

Creating a welcoming space through hospitality is not situated in the avoidance of risk. The reality is that Christian hospitality involves risks. Jayme Reaves indicated:

> The ethic of risk is rooted in the belief and practice, in essence, protective hospitality should be provided in solidarity with those who are the most vulnerable and least able to help themselves.[20]

---

17. Appendix H.
18. Corasaniti et al., "Church Massacre," para. 2.
19. Nouwen, *Reaching Out*, 10.
20. Reaves, *Safeguarding the Stranger*, loc. 4431.

A church that is filled with xenophobic persons does not exhibit the people of faith that God called us to be. For TBC, the act of extending hospitality to the LGBTQ community is a risk, not one of violence but one of communal conflict within itself. Yet, the command of Deuteronomy 10:19 was to love the stranger. Paulo Freire noted in *Pedagogy of the Oppressed* that,

> because love is an act of courage, not of fear, love is commitment to others. No matter where the oppressed are found, the act of love is commitment to their cause—the cause of liberation.[21]

The message was straightforward and clear. This sermon urged the hearers to accomplish this by reverencing the Lord, obeying the Lord's commands, loving the Lord, and serving the Lord by serving others. The audience was reminded that they, too, were strangers as slaves, segregated citizens, and targets for mass incarceration.

The sermon ended with a video clip of a CNN report showing the sentencing of Dylann Roof, the young man who killed the nine victims at the Emanuel African Methodist Episcopal Church in Charleston.[22] The participants heard the voices of the victims' relatives forgiving the young man for his actions. Having seen and heard the people of Emanuel AME openly express love and forgiveness toward a violent perpetrator, the audience was inspired to take on a similar characteristic of being a loving, inviting, and RICH church.

Sermon Five—Speaking Words of Hospitality
(John 1:1–4, 14 and 1 John 1:1–3)[23]

The Word of God is first a spoken word, an event that bears the power to create and to transform. Our testimony should give evidence to the power of the Word of God. And what the writer of the Gospel of John was able to do was to find common ground between two cultures through the Word. For the traditional Jews, the Word—the *davar*—represented the event by which heavens and earth were created. For Greeks, the Word—the *logos*—meant wisdom, which was highly valued, more so than wealth. The writer of the gospel of John used his experiences as a Hellenistic Jew to bridge the gap between the two cultures and tell them about Christ. His audience was

---

21. Freire, *Pedagogy of the Oppressed*, 89.
22. Valencia, "Shooting Victim's Kin."
23. Appendix I.

familiar with the language he used. In essence, the writer was dialogical. As members of a church in a changing community, the hearers of this sermon were challenged to use their words to create community as well. The use of RICH language can transform their world. Freire talks about the power of a true word.

> There is no true word that is not at the same time a praxis. Thus, to speak a true word is to transform the world.[24]

This sermon involved the audience in an activity in acknowledging words that may have harmed them. The goal of the activity was to demonstrate how negative and positive words may have shaped our lives because there is power in words. They can destroy as well as develop. The hearers are to address their use of destructive language in its various forms from hate speech to microaggressions. Incorporated in this message was a video clip from Oprah Winfrey's Master Class with the late author and activist, Maya Angelou.[25] She paraphrased John 1:1 and went on to talk about how negative words can eventually get into us if we are not careful. We name our world with our words, be it conscious and/or unconscious. Words shaped through our unconscious biases can become microaggressions.

As TBC strives to become more inclusive, this sermon brought the audience's attention to the importance of striving to be conscious of its microaggressions in their various forms: microinsults, microinvalidations, and microassaults. According to Sanders and Yarber in *Microaggressions in Ministry*, these are some of the hidden violent languages in the conversations of faith communities. They defined microaggressions as

> brief, everyday exchanges that send denigrating messages to certain individuals because of their group membership. These exchanges can occur in verbal, behavioral, and environmental form and communicate subtle messages of hostility, degradation, or insult based on the target's race, gender, sexual orientation, gender identity, class, ability, ethnicity, national heritage, or religion.[26]

This sermon attempted to make the hearers aware of the invisible messages that may be sent to LGBTQ persons, as well as other non-Afro-Caribbean people in their midst. In other words, it challenged them to

---

24. Freire, *Pedagogy of the Oppressed*, 87.
25. Angelou, "Power of Words."
26. Sanders and Yarber, *Microaggressions in Ministry*, 12.

tame their tongues by beginning to speak words of *love, integrity, faith,* and *encouragement*—LIFE.

For congregations like TBC, where LGBTQ people may be invisible because of DADT norms, it must be acknowledged that there is a lack of dialogue. "No real dialogue is possible between somebody and a nobody."[27] To create a hospitable and welcoming space for LGBTQ persons, there must be a liberating dialogue between TBC and those who tend to be oppressed by them.

> Because dialogue is an encounter among women and men who name the world, it must not be a situation where some name on behalf of others. It is an act of creation; it must not serve as a crafty instrument for the domination of one person by another.[28]

Love is the foundation of the words and conversation we participate in to create this environment. This sermon used a video news clip from *Good Morning America* about Antoinette Tuff, who was able to use her words to the potential school shooter Michael Brandon Hill.[29] The clip demonstrated how she used the elements of love and encouragement to communicate with Hill. Tuff's words resulted in Hill giving himself up without killing anyone. The clip embodied the synthesis of the sermon, which is to speak life into the strangers we encounter.

Sermon Six—Radical Hospitality Through Equality and Equity (Matthew 20:1–16)[30]

As I developed a close relationship with TBC, it became more evident that many within the church were manifesting the continual cycle of oppression whereby the oppressed were becoming the oppressors. The complaint of the laborers in Matthew 20:12, "You have made them equal to us," seemed to be the appropriate antithesis for this message on Jesus's concept of equality and equity through the lens of grace. This was juxtaposed with society's concept of equality for which various minorities and disenfranchised groups struggled.

---

27. Nouwen, *Reaching Out*, 92.
28. Freire, *Pedagogy of the Oppressed*, 89.
29. Tuff, "Atlanta School Shooting."
30. Appendix J.

Methodology

The sermon opened with a video clip illustration of the Parable of the Vineyard Workers that modernizes this story using the perspectives of two disgruntled White male day laborers.[31] The two workers retold the workday experience with this person who hired various work crews throughout the day to help with a construction project. What was interesting is the lack of diversity in the illustration as the cast is entirely White men. In our sociopolitical climate of "Trumpism" and the claims of the disfranchised White heterosexual male by various alt-right movements, this clip resonated with the Afro-Caribbean audience regarding their lack of employment privileges and equity.

"You have made them equal to us" is the continual claim against legislation and courts that once gave equality to former slaves, women, and now LGBTQ persons through marriage equality. The statement "You have made them equal to us" echoes some liberationists' thoughts concerning the reluctance of the Black Church and community to accept the LGBTQ community, especially when it comes to marriage equality. In its own struggle for liberation, the oppressed have become oppressors of others. In his book *Tears We Cannot Stop: A Sermon to White America*, Michael Eric Dyson gives a dialogue to this concept of the Black Church making LGBTQ persons the low members on the social class ladder:

> Black folks have blindly followed a path of prejudice that earlier ended with us as victims. Many of us find the abandonment of queer black folk a special breed of hypocrisy; failing, for the most part, to find a suitable social scapegoat for our distress, we realize there is no bottom rung that is not already occupied by another Black person, and, therefore, we make new niggers of them.[32]

He acknowledges what E. Patrick Johnson says of Black theology's refusal "to imagine that the same God who can identify with other oppressed groups—African Americans, Jews, women, etc.—can also identify with gays and lesbians."[33] The thought that the LGBTQ community can be equal with a community who believes that the path to acceptability in White America is one of piety and purity seems to be a foreign concept. Yet, inclusivity in the kingdom of God requires that all persons have access to the tree of life, regardless of their differences. Carlton Pearson, in *The Gospel of Inclusion*, says,

31. Enrico, "Parable of the Vineyard Workers."
32. Dyson, *Tears We Cannot Stop*, 162.
33. Johnson, "Feeling the Spirit," 107.

> When love, healing, and justice cease to be the cornerstones of the Christian faith, it is not the non-Christians of the world who are damned. It is Christianity itself—damned to resentment in the larger culture, to being marginalized as the domain of "right-wing wackos," to eventual extinction as a relevant force in the world.[34]

The complaint of the disgruntled day laborers served as the antithesis of the sermon as it gave the audience a perspective of equality versus equity. It argued that, like equity, God's grace strives to stand in the gap where our abilities fail us. All have indeed missed the mark and fallen short of the glory of God, yet we may need different lengths of grace extended to us to lift us from the depths of our various iniquities. As descendants of slaves, the hearers were reminded of their lack of compensation. America has not paid them well for centuries of free labor and toil. As oppressed persons of color, the audience was told that if one is oppressed, we all are oppressed. To counter this, there must be an attitude of faith as demonstrated by the day laborers who were still standing in the market toward the last work hour of the day. That faith was expressed in their availability, persistence, and hope.

Summary

The importance of authenticity and relevance was key to delivering the messages during the RICH sessions. Bryan Chapell stressed the necessity of authenticity when proclaiming the message. He says that "today pulpit excellence requires that you speak as you would naturally talk where you are fully convinced that God had charged you to deliver a life-changing, eternity-impacting message."[35] Knowing that the decision-making leaders at TBC have discussed my sexual orientation caused me to employ critical conscientization, as mentioned in *They Were Together in One Place? Toward Minority Biblical Criticism*, by Bailey, Liew, and Segovia. This became a process of "turning biblical criticism upon itself in a quest for self-awareness and self-reflection."[36] To respect the culture of DADT at TBC, I was challenged to employ a dual consciousness where the authority of the scripture and the assignment as a preacher surpassed the need to be known as a gay man. I did not hide, nor did I declare it during the preaching moments,

---

34. Pearson, *Gospel of Inclusion*, 86.
35. Chapell, *Christ-Centered Preaching*, 329.
36. Bailey et al., *Together in One Place*, xliv.

Methodology

because the messages were designed to have their preachers speak in the roles of ambassador, advocate, and ally for the stranger and voiceless persons represented in the biblical texts. Not doing so would be a complicit act of perpetuating the continual oppression and social stigmatization of the LGBTQ community. These messages declare that RICH is a call for heterosexual Christians to stop hoarding liberation for themselves and to include others.

4

Ministry Implementation, Analysis, and Evaluation

Implementation of RICH Workshops

THREE WEEKS PRIOR TO the initial session of RICH, announcements were made from the pulpit by the pastor and worship leaders. In addition, flyers were displayed through TBC, as well as handed out to Sunday worshippers. Group text messages were also sent by the pastor as reminders, and the workshop series was posted on Facebook. This promotion was necessary because I was unknown to many in the congregation. Although I had preached at TBC in prior years, the pastor made an effort to reintroduce me to the congregation as a doctoral candidate. With this in mind, it was critical to establish trust with the congregation to gain support for the RICH ministry. Given some of the internal conflict over the presence of an openly gay preacher, it was critical for TBC to see me as a member of the clergy. Therefore, I always wore my clerical collar at TBC. This would cause several of the participants to refer to me as "pastor." Furthermore, it did not cause any conflict with the pastor of TBC since we both knew that many within the Caribbean culture refer to clerical-collar-wearing ministers as "pastor" or "father" due to their Anglican and Catholic heritage.[1]

---

1. The Anglican Church is linked to British Caribbean culture through the Christianizing of slaves and the establishment of classism; yet, many Caribbean highly respect the office of clergy. This is synonymous with African Americans who have invested authority

Ministry Implementation, Analysis, and Evaluation

Though the attendance varied throughout the workshops, the promotion had a positive effect. By recording attendance, it was determined that there was a total of twenty-seven participants who attended at least one RICH session. This resulted in an overall average attendance of ten persons per session. Attendance was not taken for the Sunday worship; however, there were a total of thirty-two completed surveys.

The sessions were ninety minutes to two hours, depending on the group dynamics. Each workshop followed the program order below:

Opening Prayer
Review of Discussion Norms and Establishing a *Brave Space*[2]
Review of the Consent Forms and Confidentiality
Opening Activity
Sermonette on RICH
Activity/Discussion
Closing Prayer

All sessions, except for the Sunday sermon, were held in a small chapel in the rear of the church. The chapel consisted of a small elevated platform, lectern, and eight rows of pews. It was a well-lit room overlooking the construction site of the new apartment building behind the church. This view of the newly vacant building added to the embodiment of the importance of hospitality that was to be preached throughout the series.

During implementation, some adjustments were made to the Sermon Evaluation Questionnaire. The first questionnaire was divided into two sessions. The first fifteen statements pertained to the content of the sermon, its faithfulness to the scripture, its clarity, organization, subject matter, and momentum. The last session consisted of five statements concerning the participants' thoughts on hospitality toward specific groups as a result of hearing the message. After each session, the results were summarized and reported as averages of each section. Since this ministerial project sought to measure the transformation of the participants to be more inclusive toward LGBTQ persons, the metrics displayed in the figures are reflective of that effort only.

---

in the role of Black clergy. From the "griots" of the "invisible institutions" of slave religion to the charismatic preachers of modern megachurches, Black clergy have served the Black community in the unofficial roles of therapists, political activists, and social workers, as well as prophets and priests.

2. A brave space is a place that allows the person to speak freely, not because someone gave him or her permission to, but because the person decides to be vulnerable by putting his or her opinions out there for others to hear.

After the third session, I sought to gather more information on the transformation of the participants concerning the inclusion and advocacy of LGBTQ persons at TBC. I wanted to determine not only if people would be welcomed but also if they would be included in the various ministries. In addition, I wanted to determine if, as a result of the sermons, the participants would advocate for LGBTQ persons. Thus, two more sections of five statements each were added. This portion attempted to quantify the participants' levels of transformation regarding inclusion and advocacy of LGBTQ people in TBC. The graphs displayed in the figures show the percentage of the respondents along a spectrum of *Strongly Agreed* to *Strongly Disagreed*. These graphs also display those who chose to skip certain statements. Averages of the responses were taken and recorded in the data of this ministerial project.

Workshop One: Implementation, Analysis, and Evaluation

As participants entered the chapel, they were asked to sign in. The initial session began with prayer. There were fifteen participants, and they were asked to give their names, their role at TBC, and a brief statement about what they hope to occur in the life of the congregation. The common themes of hope were more numeric growth, spiritual growth, increased participation and commitment, and more demographic diversity within the congregation. After their sharing, the participants were asked to complete the Initial Assessment Questionnaire (appendix A). With fifteen participants, identifying as ten females and five males and all non-LGBTQ, the ethnic makeup of the group was 33 percent Black American, 56 percent Caribbean American, 6 percent Latin American, and 6 percent Asian Pacific American.[3] The age breakout was one person identifying as eighteen to twenty-five years old; one person identifying between twenty-five to thirty-eight years old; one person identifying between thirty-nine to fifty-three years old; eight persons identifying between fifty-four to seventy-two years old; and one person identifying between seventy-three years and older. Therefore, the median age of this group identified with the baby boomer generation.[4] Considering the limitations and initial guidelines established by the pastor regarding preaching and

---

3. In this section of data analysis, numeral values are used to express percentages. All other values less than one hundred are spelled out.

4. Baby Boomers are those born between 1946 and 1964 as described in Rainer and Rainer, *Millennials*, 17.

Ministry Implementation, Analysis, and Evaluation

discussing solely LGBTQ inclusion, the form was designed to consider other groups outside the norm of this Afro-Caribbean congregation.

Yet, I wanted to know about diversity within their immediate affinity circles of friends, relatives, associates, and neighbors. In addition, the questionnaire sought to determine the comfort level of inviting LGBTQ persons within those affinity groups to TBC. With this said, the affinity circles of the fifteen participants seemed somewhat diverse, with several participants acknowledging LGBTQ persons (figure 1).

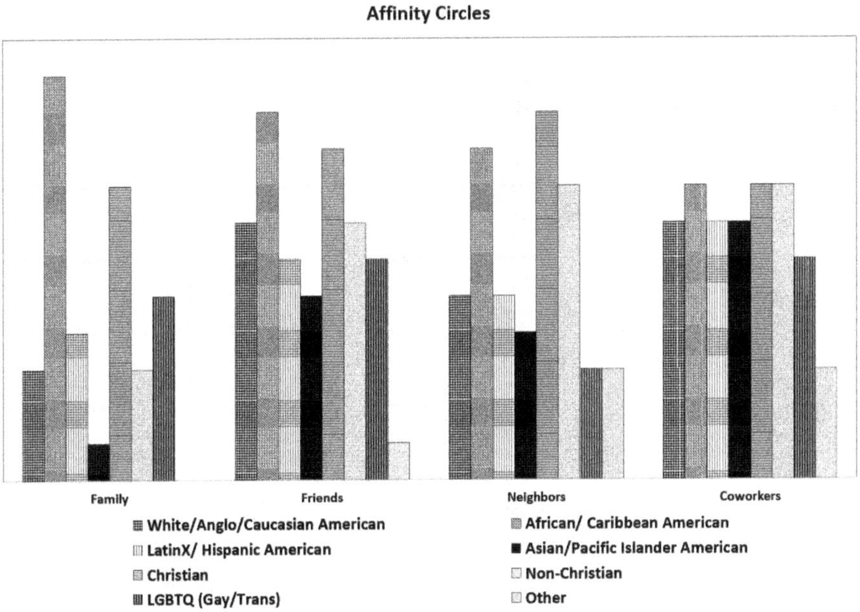

Affinity Circles

▨ White/Anglo/Caucasian American	▨ African/ Caribbean American
▥ LatinX/ Hispanic American	■ Asian/Pacific Islander American
▨ Christian	☐ Non-Christian
▮ LGBTQ (Gay/Trans)	☐ Other

Figure 1. Assessment Results of Affinity Circles

When asked the question about the likelihood of inviting particular people of those circles to TBC, it was quite revealing to learn that, although many knew LGBTQ persons, they were not comfortable with inviting them to TBC (figure 2). In fact, the LGBTQ group ranked similarly to the Non-Christian category of people whom the participants would not be likely to invite to worship at TBC.

R.I.C.H. in Preaching

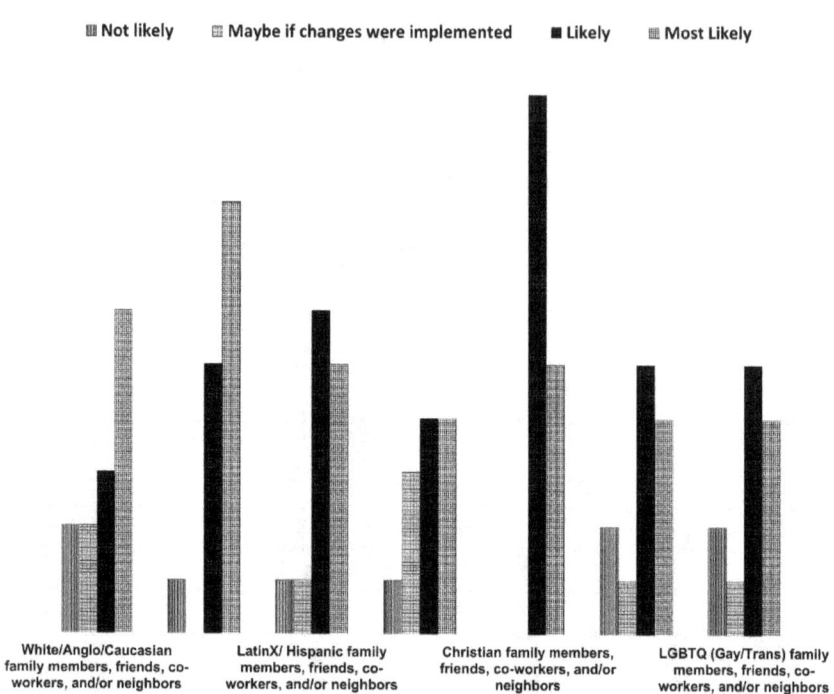

Figure 2. Assessment Results of Inviting Others

The questionnaire asked about the treatment of persons at TBC in terms of equality, beginning with the participants' opinions about how specific groups of people should be treated at TBC. The group agreed that regardless of race, gender, sexual identity, age, and physical ability, all persons should be treated equally, with perhaps more consideration given to the elderly and physically disabled (figure 3).

Ministry Implementation, Analysis, and Evaluation

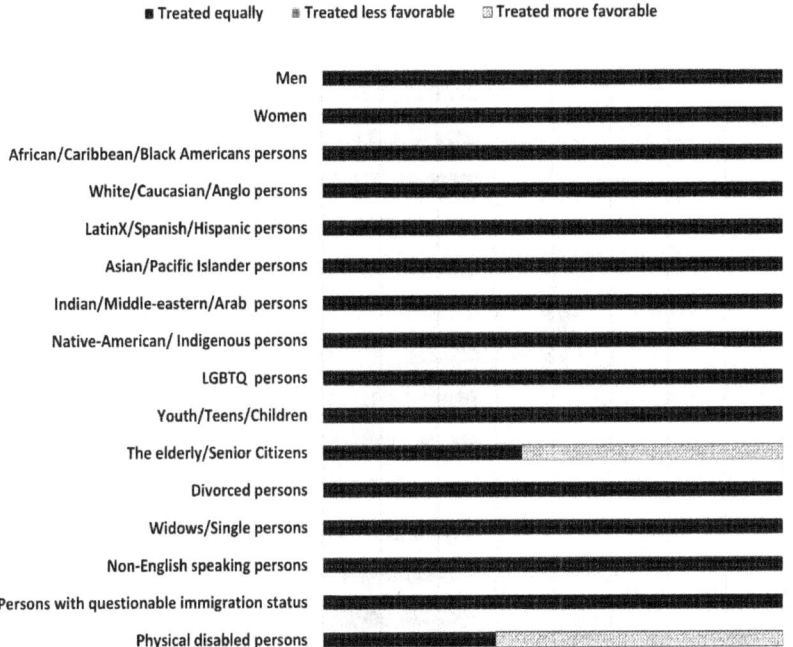

Figure 3. Assessment of Ideal Equality at TBC

Yet, according to some of the participants, the treatment of certain persons, especially those who are LGBTQ, is less favorable in terms of equality, while only a small percentage thought they were treated more favorably (figure 4).

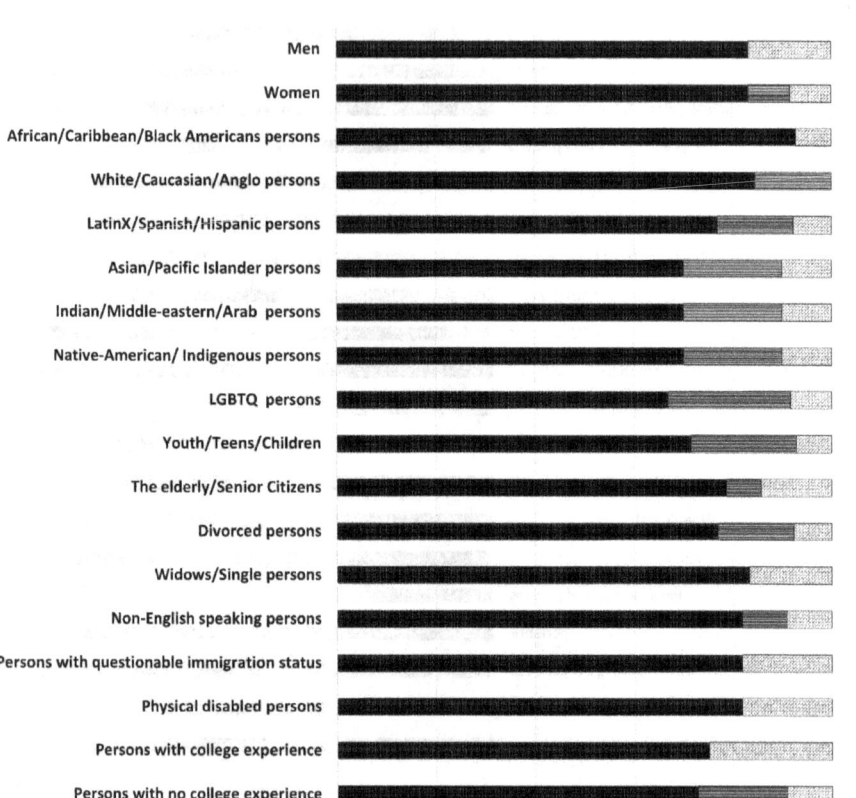

Figure 4. Assessment of Actual Perception of Equality at TBC

In terms of issues of diversity and inclusion, the questionnaire posed several questions regarding the participants' thoughts about TBC. For the purpose of this ministerial project, I only analyzed those questions with implications toward the LGBTQ community. Those questions yield the following responses in figure 5.

In terms of sexuality and gender, Trinity is a place that welcomes all people in worship.

Strongly Agree	Agree	Disagree	Strongly Disagree	Not Applicable	Neutral	Skipped
20%	33%	27%	0%	0%	0%	20%

In terms of sexuality and gender, Trinity is a place that includes all people in leadership and decision making.

Strongly Agree	Agree	Disagree	Strongly Disagree	Not Applicable	Neutral	Skipped
7%	27%	27%	0%	0%	0%	40%

The church welcomes and accepts all people regardless of any person's race, sexual orientation, gender identity, HIV status, age, ability, gender or ethnicity.

Strongly Agree	Agree	Disagree	Strongly Disagree	Not Applicable	Neutral	Skipped
27%	33%	13%	0%	0%	0%	27%

There are no negative repercussions for someone who voices concerns and comments about diversity and inclusion issues within Trinity.

Strongly Agree	Agree	Disagree	Strongly Disagree	Not Applicable	Neutral	Skipped
20%	40%	13%	0%	0%	0%	27%

Trinity welcomes discussion pertaining to differences and uniqueness within its body.

Strongly Agree	Agree	Disagree	Strongly Disagree	Not Applicable	Neutral	Skipped
20%	27%	13%	0%	7%	7%	27%

The leadership of Trinity responds to concerns and comments about the diversity and inclusion issues in a respectful and timely manner.

Strongly Agree	Agree	Disagree	Strongly Disagree	Not Applicable	Neutral	Skipped
13%	33%	20%	0%	0%	7%	27%

Jokes and disparaging remarks about race, ethnicity, gender, physical ability, age, HIV status, sexual orientation and / or gender identity are not tolerated in Trinity.

Strongly Agree	Agree	Disagree	Strongly Disagree	Not Applicable	Neutral	Skipped
33%	27%	0%	0%	0%	7%	33%

People of diverse races, sexual orientations, genders, gender identities, ages, physical abilities, ethnicities, and HIV status are comfortable worshipping at Trinity.

Strongly Agree	Agree	Disagree	Strongly Disagree	Not Applicable	Neutral	Skipped
33%	33%	7%	0%	0%	0%	27%

Trinity has no unspoken rules and makes no assumptions about diverse races, sexual orientations, genders, gender identities, ages, physical abilities, ethnicities, and HIV status that could affect the worship environment.

Strongly Agree	Agree	Disagree	Strongly Disagree	Not Applicable	Neutral	Skipped
20%	40%	13%	0%	0%	0%	27%

Figure 5. Table Assessment for Inclusion at TBC

The results revealed that a portion of the participants clearly disagreed with the statement that TBC is welcoming and inclusive of all persons. In addition, a portion of those who participated chose to skip the questions. The act of skipping questions became a regular pattern among the participants. This was later mentioned in the group discussions. The participants' response to the pattern of skipping questions revealed their level of discomfort with disclosing their real opinions about issues regarding LBGTQ persons and inclusion at TBC. That will be shared in the following chapter.

After the participants completed the Initial Assessment Questionnaire, I established norms for discussions. The participants were encouraged to be open, reflect deeply, listen carefully, remain flexible, and promote safety. This was to establish a safe space for sharing ideas, as well as a brave space for challenging each other. In addition, each person was encouraged to participate in the conversation but not to dominate it. All participants agreed. The norms were reviewed in each workshop session.

The participants were led in an individual activity where they were told to list six to eight people whom they trust; however, these persons could not be relatives by blood and/or marriage. Then the participants were asked to place a check by the name(s) of those listed who fell into the following categories: those who are of the same gender and sex as yourself, those who are of the same race as yourself, those who share the same faith/religion as yourself, those who are within eight to ten years of your age. After the completion of the question, the participants were asked if there were names on their lists that did not have a check. No one had any. Then a poll was taken to determine how many persons had checks next by someone's name. Only two persons had names listed where there were at least two checks by them. The goal of the exercise was to help the participants establish the degree of diversity or lack of it within their own affinity groups and to see how trusting they were of people who were different from themselves.

The exercise served well to introduce Acts 10:34–43 and the sermon entitled "A Vision to Rise Up" (appendix E). Using the Apostle Peter as an example of someone willing to confront his prejudices and biases against the Gentiles, I issued the call for the hearers to rise above their levels of comfort, resist their biases, and receive others through hospitality.

The sermon was followed with another activity whereby the group was shown four images of potential visitors to TBC:

1. a Black heterosexual couple with two children
2. a Black, elderly heterosexual couple with one person in a wheelchair
3. an interracial heterosexual couple
4. a Black female same-sex couple with two children

Without any descriptions for any image, the group was asked what opportunities and/or barriers exist at TBC for these potential visitors. For the

Ministry Implementation, Analysis, and Evaluation

same-sex couple, the audience initially responded with difficulty in determining the gender of both. The responses varied but most agreed with one participant's comment: "At TBC there may not be many opportunities for them because some would have issues because they are a same-sex couple." When asked whether the couple would still be welcome at TBC, the group indicated that some would welcome them, but others may find it unsettling.

At the end of the final activity, the participants completed a Sermon Evaluation Questionnaire (appendix C). For the first fifteen statements—which dealt with the sermon's faithfulness to scripture, its clarity, engagement, outline, momentum, and ability to capture the participants' attention—on overall an average 69 percent of the participants Strongly Agreed with the statements, while an average 27 percent Agreed. The remaining average of 4 percent represents the participants who chose to skip some of the questions.

As a result of hearing the message, the participants responded thusly in figure 6. The data showed that the participants thought that TBC should be a welcoming environment for all people regardless of age, abilities, gender identity, HIV status, sexual orientation, and race.

Workshop Two: Implementation, Analysis, and Evaluation

Similar to the initial workshop, participants entered the chapel and signed in. There were six participants. I learned later that the participating deaconesses had to attend a local conference. We began with prayer, then reviewed the agenda. I conducted a small review of the last session and proceeded to lead the group in an activity. TBC had promoted a Homecoming Sunday to encourage its members to invite family, friends, and non-active members to the church. Using this occasion, I showed the audience five photos of different persons:

1. a Latinx or multiracial male
2. an interracial couple with two children
3. a Black female wearing a hijab
4. a Black male with dreadlocks
5. a male same-sex couple with three children

R.I.C.H. in Preaching

Figure 6. Questionnaire Results for Sermon One.

The task for the group was to pretend to invite each person(s) to TBC by completing the following statement: "The reason you should come and visit TBC is . . ." The participants wrote their statements down privately. Upon completion, the group was led in a discussion focusing on the following

Ministry Implementation, Analysis, and Evaluation

questions: Did your statement change with your perception of the person/people you saw in the picture to invite? What opportunities at TBC did you emphasize? What obstacles at TBC or within yourself affected and/or prevented you from inviting the person/people? The participants offered a variety of responses, acknowledging that for the same-sex couple the statement may change to emphasize that TBC is an inclusive church. No one offered statements that the couple would not be invited but rather that they would emphasize inclusivity.

The activity served as the preamble to the scripture of Luke 10:25–37, about the Good Samaritan, whereby the hearers were challenged to see themselves showing mercy to others and providing continual care as the innkeeper. Following the sermon, I asked the participants to identify ministries at TBC that function as a paradigm of the Good Samaritan and to identify those activities that function as the innkeeper. The participants identified their clothing ministries, community picnic night out, shopping trips, Blankets of Love ministries, Project Jamaica, Anchor House Women's Shelter, and Bergen Street Shelter for Men as opportunities for doing the work of the Good Samaritan. For innkeeper ministries, they identified the following: Project Unity Bible Study, community movie nights, prayer breakfasts, senior citizens' ministries, and their after-church hospitality hour. I then asked the question of whether or not a person's race, sexual identity, gender, social class, or religion was a prerequisite for participation in any of the various ministries and activities. The participants replied, "Certainly not." However, they all agreed that there are opportunities for them to improve consistency in their ministries and processes for greeting and receiving visitors and new members at TBC.

The participants completed the Sermon Evaluation Questionnaire. For the message itself, an average of 93.3 percent of the participants Strongly Agreed with the message's content being faithful to scripture, clear, engaging, flowing, and understandable; an average of 4.4 percent Agreed, and an average of 2.2 percent skipped some of the questions. As a result of the message, the participants were in one hundred percent agreement concerning the inclusion of people regardless of age, ability, HIV status, gender identity, sexual orientation, and race (figure 7).

R.I.C.H. in Preaching

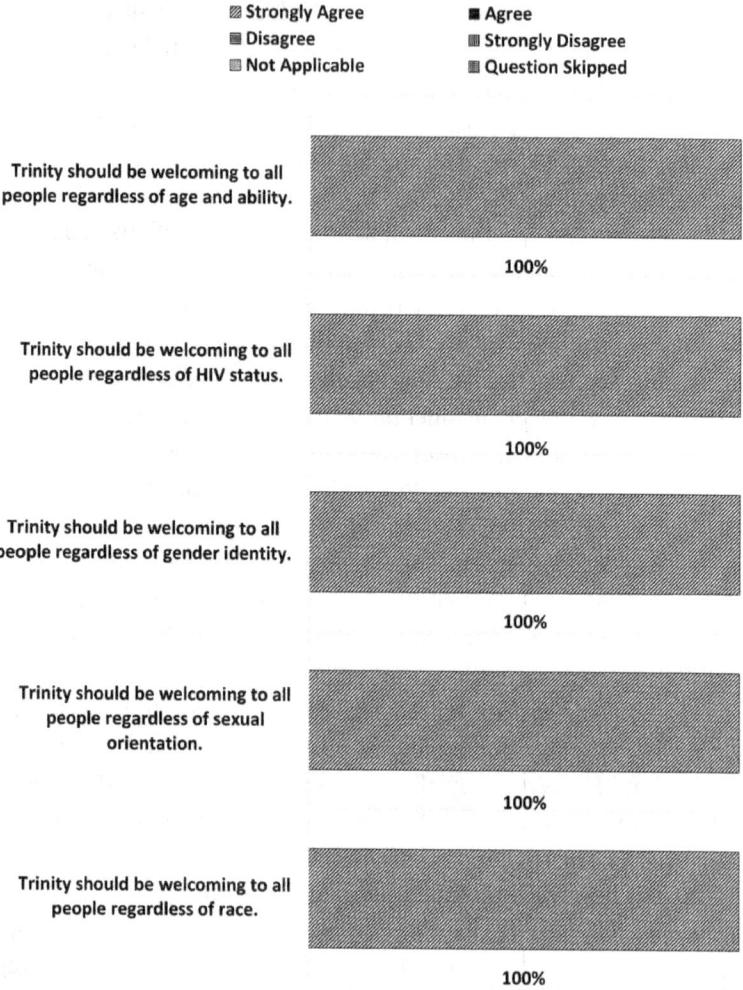

Figure 7. Questionnaire Results for Sermon Two

Workshop Three: Implementation, Analysis, and Evaluation

Until now, the pastor had attended the workshops, but due to a scheduling conflict, he could not attend this one. There were nine in attendance, with one new participant. After prayer, a review of the agenda, consent forms,

Ministry Implementation, Analysis, and Evaluation

and norms, I introduced a video clip concerning the impact of the church with the Reverend A. R. Bernard, pastor of the Christian Culture Center.[5] The clip shows Bernard responding to the question about millennials leaving the church. He indicates that if the church measures its success by numbers rather than its impact on history, as well as the community, it will lose a generation. The activity for the participants was to discuss ways in which TBC impacts its community. The group responded by listing several of the church's ministries and activities, as they did in workshop two, such as the homeless ministry and movie night, as well as collaborations with other community organizations. This activity was followed by another video clip from the PBS News Hour of Casper ter Kuile,[6] a millennial and researcher at Harvard University, offering a monologue on why he left the church and found community elsewhere. He argues that millennials like himself hunger for authentic connection and community. After the clip, the participants were asked to discuss ways in which TBC creates community. The goal of both exercises was to have the participants examine their abilities to establish relationships with millennials.

The activities concerning millennials and the church served to introduce the sermon "Radical Inclusive Christian Hospitality in Worship," based on Revelation 7:9–17. The sermon echoed the video clips about millennials being a diverse generation and pointed out that the church lacked diversity and inclusiveness. After the sermon, the group viewed a video clip of Trillia Newbell, author of *God's Very Good Idea*, explaining that diversity in the church is more than race.[7] Due to time constraints, the group was asked to privately reflect on the video in preparation for the next session. One participant verbally noted in front of the group that the message was thought-provoking and had many points that could cause division and make it difficult for TBC to become inclusive. The participant went on to note that some mindsets would be difficult to change. The participants completed the Sermon Evaluation Questionnaire. For the message itself, an average of 66 percent Strongly Agreed with the message's content being faithful to scripture, clear, engaging, flowing, and understandable; an average of 30 percent Agreed, and an average of 4 percent skipped some of the questions. As a result of the message, an average of 83 percent Strongly Agreed that TBC should be welcoming to all people regardless of race,

---

5. Skeldon, "Millennial."
6. Kuile, "Millennials."
7. Newbell, "Why Diversity."

sexual orientation, gender identity, HIV status, age, and ability. I found it interesting that 25 percent of the participants chose to skip the question on sexual orientation (figure 8).

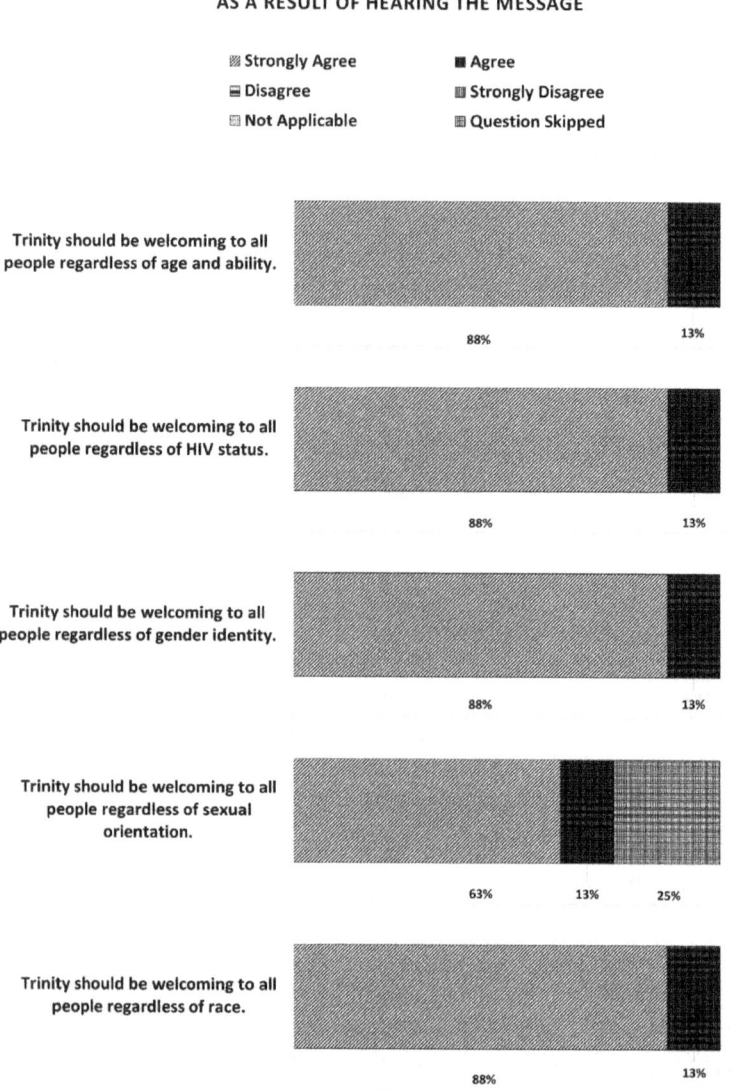

Figure 8. Questionnaire Results for Sermon Three

Workshop Four: Implementation, Analysis, and Evaluation

As planned, due to the holiday schedule of the church, this workshop took place one month later. The task was to conduct a review of the previous subject matter to refresh the participants' memories and introduce the sermon topic for the session. There were eleven participants. As with the prior sessions, the workshop began with prayer, review of the agenda, group norms, review of consent forms, and prior subject material. Afterward, the sermon message was introduced. Unlike the prior sessions, I did not lead the group in activity prior to the sermon. The message for this workshop was "Loving the Stranger in a Culture of Fear," with Deuteronomy 10:12–19 serving as the scripture. The message ended with the video clip of the sentencing of Dylann Roof, where the family members of his victims offered statements of forgiveness and love. The RICH participants were visually affected and offered other examples of radical forgiveness.

The sermon was followed by a group activity where the participants watched a video clip concerning the ways churches tell newcomers they are not wanted,[8] and a video clip about the six most essential minutes for newcomers.[9] The goal was for the participants to compare those words of caution to their processes at TBC. The participants were asked to complete the revised Sermon Evaluation Questionnaire. The pastor of TBC and I reminded them not to skip any of the questions. For the message itself, an average of 85 percent Strongly Agreed with the message's content being faithful to scripture, clear, engaging, flowing, and understandable, and an average 15 percent Agreed. In terms of hospitality, an average of 78 percent Strongly Agreed that TBC should be welcoming to all people regardless of race, sexual orientation, gender identity, HIV status, age, and ability. An average of 22 percent Agreed. For the new statements on inclusion, an average of 62 percent Strongly Agreed that TBC should offer opportunities for all persons to participate in ministries, committees, and leadership regardless of race, sexual orientation, race, gender identity, HIV status, and physical ability. For the new statements on advocacy, an average of 77 percent Strongly Agreed that they would advocate for the inclusion of all persons to be welcomed regardless of race, immigration status, sexual orientation, gender identity, HIV status, age, and ability; an

---

8. Hawkins, "Church Hospitality."
9. Logue, "6 Minutes."

average of 18 percent Agreed, and an average of 9 percent Disagreed with the statement (figure 9).

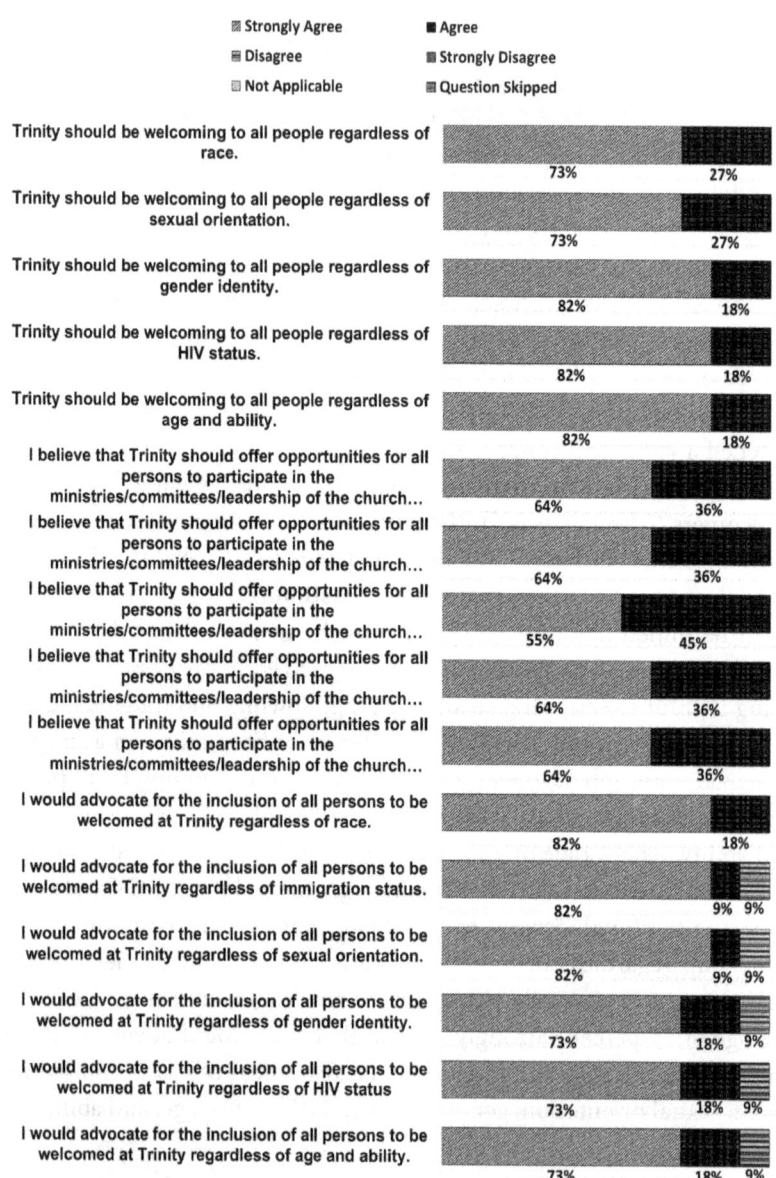

Figure 9. Questionnaire Results for Sermon Four

Ministry Implementation, Analysis, and Evaluation

Sermon on Sunday Morning: Implementation, Analysis, and Evaluation

Initially, I planned to do a workshop; however, the participants and pastor of TBC desired to have more of the TBC members hear and see a message on RICH. Therefore, the pastor requested that I preach a Sunday sermon incorporating the media of PowerPoint. This sermon was preached in the main sanctuary. The sermon title was "Speaking Words of Hospitality," using John 1:1–4, 14; and 1 John 1:1–3. I learned after the sermon that the congregation had their annual meeting the day before, during which harsh words were shared among the attendees. Therefore, this message was timely.

After the sermon, while the pastor was extending the invitation to Christ, an elderly woman whom many consider to be the mother of the church asked permission to come to the front of the church and address the congregation. The pastor conceded. The elderly woman, who declared her age to be ninety years old, stated how much she enjoyed the message and the importance of TBC to hearken to the theme of it and begin to speak words of LIFE (love, integrity, faith, and encouragement) to each other. She affirmed me not only as a servant of God but a "holy man." For the thirty-two attendees who completed the Sermon Evaluation Questionnaire, an average of 82 percent Strongly Agreed with the message's content being faithful to scripture, clear, engaging, flowing, and understandable; and an average 15 percent Agreed; while an average 3 percent skipped questions. In terms of hospitality, an average of 88 percent Strongly Agreed that TBC should be welcoming to all people regardless of race, sexual orientation, gender identity, HIV status, age, and ability. An average of 10 percent Agreed. Three percent skipped the questions. For the statements on inclusion, an average of 49 percent Strongly Agreed that TBC should offer opportunities for all persons to participate in the ministries, committees, and leadership regardless of race, sexual orientation, gender identity, HIV status, and physical ability. An average of 35 percent Agreed. An average of 16 percent skipped the questions. For the statements on advocacy, an average of 61 percent Strongly Agreed that they would advocate for the inclusion of all persons to be welcomed regardless of race, immigration status, sexual orientation, gender identity, HIV status, age, and ability; an average of 23 percent Agreed, and an average of 16 percent skipped the questions (figure 10).

R.I.C.H. in Preaching

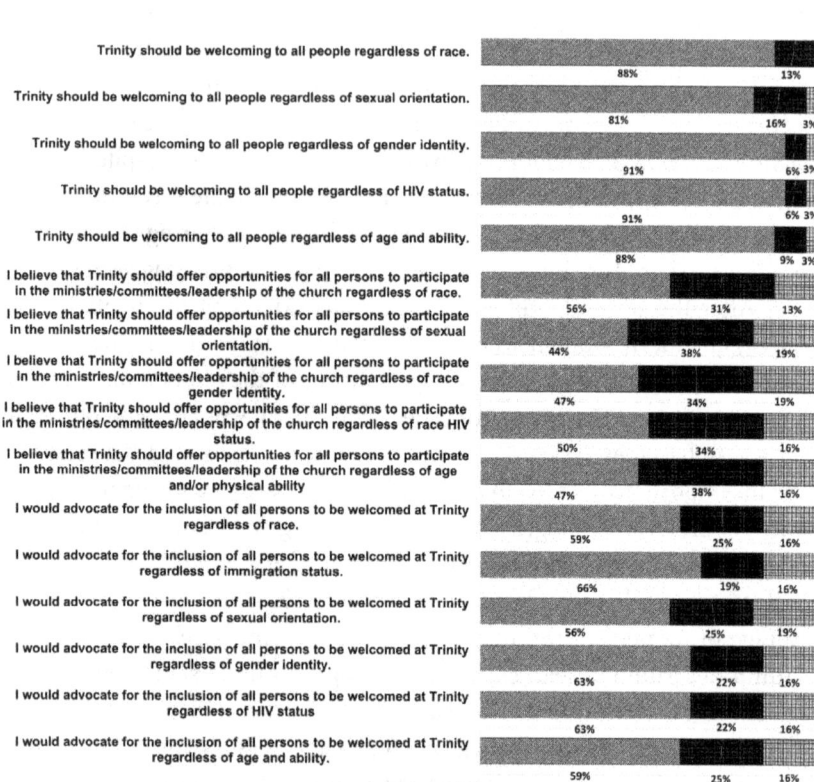

Figure 10. Questionnaire Results from Sermon Five

Several participants added comments to their surveys. "I believe in Deuteronomy!" was written on one survey where the questions regarding sexual orientation were skipped. One person noted that s/he was not sure about including LGBTQ persons in leadership. Another wrote a comment pertaining to the sermon itself: "I was blessed. I cried."

Workshop Five: Implementation, Analysis, and Evaluation

This was the last workshop that involved preaching a sermon. Also, the session was designed to allow time for a group discussion. Otherwise, the session followed the same order as previous sessions. There were eleven

Ministry Implementation, Analysis, and Evaluation

attendees. The pastor was absent from the session due to a scheduling conflict. Also, it should be noted that, since the implementation of the workshops, this is the first time that the sounds from the construction workers on the new apartment building next door could be clearly heard. The hammers and construction tools were loud, but not so loud that it interrupted the session. In fact, the sound helped to embody the message of the sermon concerning God's equity toward those laboring in the kingdom. The attendees at RICH acknowledged the coincidence of the hammers as they read aloud the passage in Matthew 20:1–16. Furthermore, the video clip of the day laborers working on a construction site drew a humorous response from the audience. The message was entitled "Radical Hospitality through Equality and Equity."

After the preached Word, the group was led into a discussion about equality and equity at TBC. The participants were shown a diagram of the results of their initial assessment pertaining to the equal treatment of people at TBC (figure 3). It was noted that all respondents in the assessment felt that individuals, regardless of race, gender, sexual identity, age, and various ability should be treated equally. Yet, not all felt that individuals were actually being treated equally (figure 4). This disparity served as the basis for the group discussion that followed. The participants were asked to gather into four groups and discuss the following four questions:

1. What are your initial thoughts on the disagreement about how people are treated at TBC? How is that inequality communicated in TBC? What are the internal structures and practices that may promote inequality?

2. There was a pattern for some participants to skip questions, especially those questions dealing with LGBTQ persons. What would be some of the possible reasons for this? Are people not comfortable dealing with those types of questions?

3. It has been stated during these training sessions that there may be some persons or groups within TBC that would not be hospitable to LGBTQ persons. How do you propose that TBC can overcome that and become more inclusive?

4. How have these sessions and sermons changed and/or reinforced your beliefs about inclusivity within the church?

Once participants chose their groups, each group selected a reporter to speak on its behalf. The participants were given approximately twelve minutes to discuss. Once the time was called, I asked each group to report its thoughts.

Beginning with the first set of questions, group one replied that it did not observe any inequality in TBC. As leaders, they felt they treated people equally. Furthermore, they felt that hospitality works both ways between hosts and visitors. Group two noted that they desired to see TBC become more diverse and open to others. They did not feel that TBC treated people equally. Group three felt that inequality is sometimes subtle and sometimes blatantly displayed at TBC. There is often a lack of interaction among people. Group four said that if persons did not have a social position, affluence, and money, they did not get attention. They did note that there is a mentality that people with status are regarded highly. All the groups noted that there are some structures that hinder equality, such as the separation of the deacons and deaconesses and the gender-based assigned seating of the two boards in the church. They recalled having discussions about doing away with the separation.

For the second set of questions, group one noted that people did not want to face the issue. People may not accept LGBTQ people and did not want to put it in writing. They noted that individuals like that are inauthentic and insincere.

Group two noted that people may still be struggling with the issues. They noted their own struggle and growth in accepting LGBTQ people. One participant said:

> It used to be that if I knew that a church had a gay preacher, I would avoid going there. But as I matured in my Christian walk, I've come to the conclusion that people are people and sin is sin: black, yellow, white, pink, big, or small. Who am I to judge others? The Bible says by the same measure we judge others so we will be judged. I'm going to love you for who you are.

Group three noted that the church lacked the forum to discuss the *isms* and the phobias about homosexuality. They added that, for some, the Black Church has struggled with eliminating stereotypes and stigmas about Black identity and sexuality. For these reasons, there may be resistance to adding the LGBTQ label. The group talked about how people have historically been forced to leave the church because of teenage pregnancy and sexual identity.

Group four noted that the issue of homosexuality has been present in TBC for years. They indicated that they knew prior people in the church

Ministry Implementation, Analysis, and Evaluation

that were homosexuals, and it was never discussed. They accepted them, but no one talked about their sexuality. One participant noted that she had a problem with people making distinctions between straight and gay persons because, regardless of sexuality, we all are children of God. She could not understand why LGBTQ persons would fight to march in Christian parades, such as the St. Patrick Day Parade. After noting that she had co-workers who were gay, this participant said, "Years ago in society, not too many people talked about gay issues." I used this as an educational moment and responded to the group that such a fight was about inclusion and identity. People want to be seen in their wholeness. They want their lives and struggles to be as acknowledged as others.

Interestingly, participants began to engage more in open discussion. One participant responded to group four:

> Just because prior gay people were at TBC and no one said anything outright about it, did not mean that people did not harbor resentment or hostility about those persons' sexuality.

The participant added that there might have been other contributing factors that allowed TBC to welcome those persons, such as prominent social positions, college education, and finances. The group indicated that homophobia is prevalent in the Caribbean culture as well as Black America, and until persons receive sensitivity training and are exposed to other diverse groups, they may hold on to a limited perspective of gay people. One participant recalled her first encounter with what she thought was a gay child but later learned that the child was gender nonconforming.

Due to the in-depth positive conversation among the groups sharing their stories of struggle with LGBTQ acceptance, I posed this final question: What do you think we need to do at TBC to continue discussions about inclusion? One participant noted that mental illness and health should be included in the conversation about including people with varying abilities.

As we closed, the group applauded and noted that the church should have more dialogue about issues such as this. The participants completed their Sermon Evaluation Questionnaires. The responses as they pertained to hospitality, inclusion, and advocacy are in figure 11. An average 69 percent Strongly Agreed with the message's content being faithful to scripture, clear, engaging, flowing, and understandable; and an average 31 percent Agreed. In terms of hospitality, an average of 62 percent Strongly Agreed that TBC should be welcoming to all people regardless of race, sexual orientation, gender identity, HIV status, age, and ability; while an average of

38 percent Agreed. For the statements on inclusion, an average of 40 percent Strongly Agreed that TBC should offer opportunities for all persons to participate in the ministries, committees, and leadership regardless of race, sexual orientation, race, gender identity, HIV status, and physical ability. An average of 58 percent Agreed, and an average of 2 percent Disagreed. For the 2 percent disagreement, further detail revealed that this disagreement dealt with persons' HIV status and inclusion. For the statements on advocacy, an average of 59 percent Strongly Agreed that they would advocate for the inclusion of all persons to be welcomed regardless of race, immigration status, sexual orientation, gender identity, HIV status, age, and ability; an average of 41 percent Agreed. It should be noted that there were not any skipped questions.

Implementation of One-On-One Interviews

Four participants in RICH were selected to interview.[10] In addition, a final interview and debriefing took place with the pastor of TBC. With the consent of each participant, the interviews were recorded for later review and documentation. With the pastor's permission, each interview was conducted in his private study. All interviews took place after a workshop or Sunday service at the convenience of the participant. Although a set list of questions was prepared, I used an open-ended approach to facilitate the conversation and allow participants to share their own stories as they related to inclusive hospitality to LGBTQ persons. Because many of the interviewees were concerned about confidentiality, there is a minimum description of the participant. The identities of the participants were labeled as RICH-1, RICH-2, RICH-3, and RICH-4, with the exception of the pastor of TBC and me. I am labeled as the researcher. Furthermore, the Caribbean dialect and colloquialisms of some participants were paraphrased and redacted to protect their identity and to provide clarity in reading the dialogue. All interviews may be found in appendix K.

The interview with RICH-1 took place after I preached the Sunday sermon entitled "Speaking Words of Hospitality." The participant was a Jamaican female, part of the ministerial leadership team at TBC, and between the age range of sixty to sixty-five years old. In this interview, she shared insight into the history of the DADT culture at TBC and its previous encounters with members of the LGBTQ community. The interview revealed that as long as

10. Appendix K.

Ministry Implementation, Analysis, and Evaluation

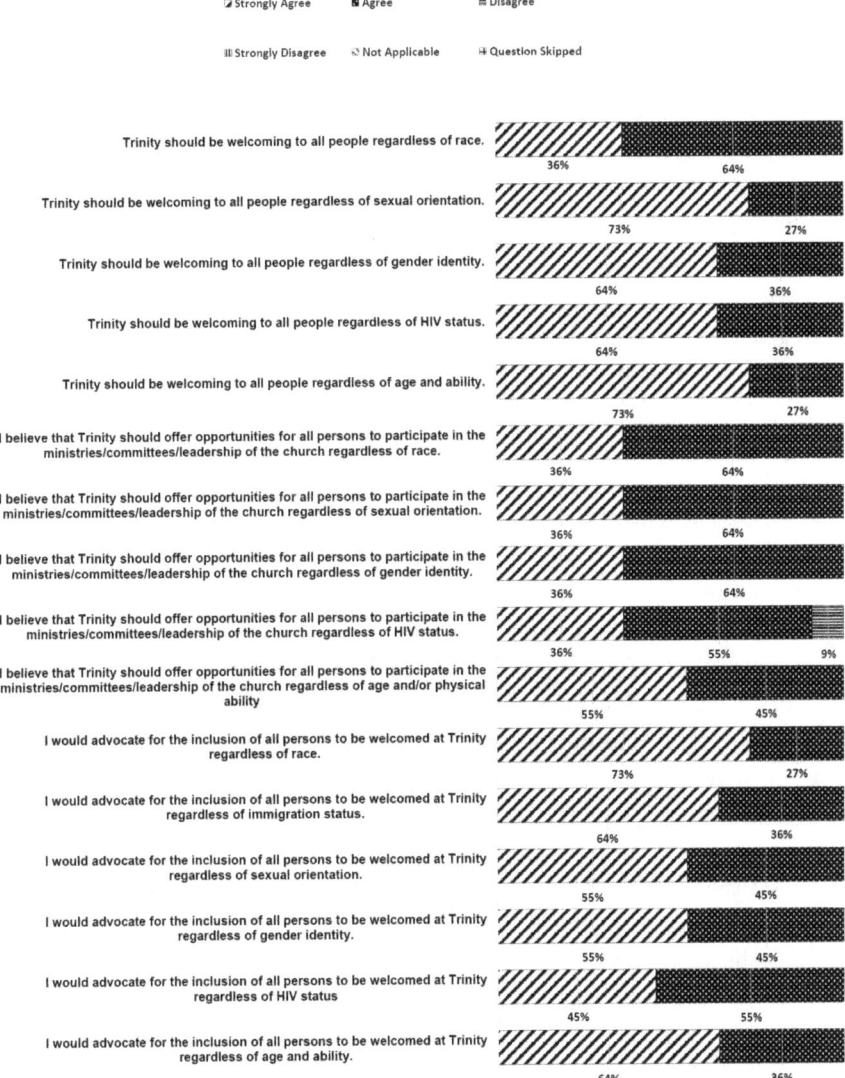

Figure 11. Questionnaire Results for Sermon Six.

LGBTQ persons were not open about their sexuality, acceptance within TBC was possible. When that code was broken, whether through discovery or conversation, there was some conflict. The interviewee indicated that although no one directly reprimanded LGBTQ persons, their continual presence

R.I.C.H. in Preaching

seemed to have brought discord with a few dissenters. RICH-1 disclosed the fact that during that time, there were few advocates to combat the dissension.

The day after the sermon "Hospitality through Equality and Equity," I conducted an interview with RICH-2. This interviewee expressed concerns for confidentiality because many within TBC did not know her personal story about dealing with a grandchild who was in the process of transitioning his gender. The interview with RICH-2 revealed that there were no resources within TBC for the families of LGBTQ persons to learn about loving and helping their loved ones with coming out, transitioning, and finding community. As a grandparent, RICH-2 reached out to me for information because of my openness as a gay minister whom she seemed to trust to give her credible information about the issue. The sermons on inclusion and acceptance, as well as embodying the LGBTQ Christian perspective, helped this interviewee move from a place of secrecy to one of safety and hopefulness. She received positive reinforcement about loving her grandchild in spite of the culture of homophobia with which she was familiar.

After the final workshop and sermon on RICH, the interview with RICH-3 occurred. She was a Latin-American female between sixty-five and seventy years old and a member of the leadership board. The interviewee shared about her previous experience at another church, which was predominately White and what she encountered when she initially began attending TBC. She further shared her observations about the spiritual growth of TBC and how the sermons caused her to think about some of the policies and procedures in TBC pertaining to welcoming and recruiting newcomers. Organizationally, she hopes to see TBC change some of its internal structures so that newcomers can sense and discern the inclusivity within the church. As a leader on the executive board of the church, she noted how she has advocated for the inclusion of others and that the messages she heard through this ministerial project have affirmed her actions.

The interview with RICH-4 was a sensitive one. So, the particulars of the participant's identity were protected. For this ministerial project, the plural pronouns—they, their, and them—were used to hide the gender of the interviewee. It was an interview that occurred after the sermon on "Hospitality through Equality and Equity." The interviewee expressed the desire to voice "their" struggle with their sexual orientation as an LGBTQ person in a heterosexual marriage. The DADT culture and role of the interviewee at TBC have precluded a "safe space" for them to discuss their struggles with homosexuality. However, the messages preached about

Ministry Implementation, Analysis, and Evaluation

RICH have encouraged the interviewee to conduct a self-evaluation of their identity and purpose. The desire to live an authentic life of sexual expression was important to RICH-4.

I conducted an interview with the pastor prior to the final discussion and group interview with the RICH participants. We discussed many of the recurring themes of DADT concerning TBC's interaction with previous LGBTQ members. He knew why some left and confirmed the following: one person left after his same-sex marriage, and it was discovered, and persons in leadership expressed their dissent. This person chose to leave on his own to avoid discord. And, a second person would leave because they wanted to live their life openly and not be reduced to DADT culture. For the second person, the pastor indicated that many within TBC felt a sense of loss since they provided various forms of assistance to this person. Since the implementation of RICH, the transformation of the participants at TBC has taken him by surprise. He stated that some of his leaders have begun to disclosed information regarding LGBTQ family members and friends. He also acknowledged that the DADT culture had prevented people from authentic conversations and community. In addition, the leaders at TBC have spoken favorably about RICH and my presence at TBC. They desired to see the continuation of RICH after the ministerial project is done. He declared that transformation occurred because of my embodiment of the queer community through preaching. Finally, it would be agreed that during the final group discussion and interview, I would talk openly about my journey as a gay minister, thus breaking the DADT of TBC.

Closing Group Discussion and Interview: Implementation, Analysis, and Evaluation

Prior to the final session, it was decided to push the study further by breaking the DADT culture of TBC and share my story about coming out while being the pastor at Cross of Life Lutheran Church. This was determined after the previous group discussion and hearing some of the similar themes of secrecy in the interviews. This plan was shared with the pastor, who agreed.

This session would be a summary review of the previous topics and include a focus-led group interview. The passages used for the session were 1 Corinthians 13:4–8; John 15:12–17; and 1 John 4:8. The leading question for the overall discussion was "Who can the church love?" The participants were presented with data from the Pew Research Center, showing that 81

R.I.C.H. in Preaching

percent of millennials supported marriage equality. They were also shown Bishop T. D. Jakes's response to the *HuffPost* regarding the church's evolving stance on LGBTQ issues stating that each church should have a theological discussion about its position with the queer community. The objective was to lead TBC participants in such a discussion regarding their views of the LGBTQ community. Two video clips from a panel discussion at Columbia University regarding the role of the Black Church in the United States were shown.[11] The first clip was of Rev. Otis Moss III, pastor of Trinity United Church of Christ in Chicago, Illinois, speaking about the Black Church's struggle with faith and love. The second clip showed Professor Anthea Butler, the Associate Professor and Graduate Chair of Religion at the University of Pennsylvania, discussing the exodus of Black millennials from churches lacking an authentic love practice. Afterward, the participants were shown a composite of the responses to the Initial Assessment Questionnaire (figure 5) regarding inclusion and hospitality at TBC. This was in the form of a bar graph (figure 12) to show the group the variance in their opinions. This was used to show the participants their struggle between a practice of fundamentalism and the practice of loving others as themselves.

Immediately after this, I shared my personal journey as a pastor of an Afro-Caribbean church and the church's journey toward inclusive hospitality. Then the group was asked to read aloud 1 Corinthian 13:4–8. The participants were then asked to break into three discussion groups and address the following questions:

1. Can you give concrete examples of how TBC is patient and kind to persons who are neither Afro-Caribbean nor heterosexual in its congregation and/or community?
2. Are there examples where TBC has been or currently is arrogant or rude to those who are not Afro-Caribbean heterosexual men?
3. When new people come to TBC, are there examples of how the members of TBC welcome their new ideas and do not insist on their own traditional ways?
4. What happens if members become irritable or resentful and leave because things do not go their way?

Given ten minutes, the participants had to choose a leader to serve as a reporter for their results. Some groups struggled with the exercise, but

---

11. Glaude et al., "Black Church."

Ministry Implementation, Analysis, and Evaluation

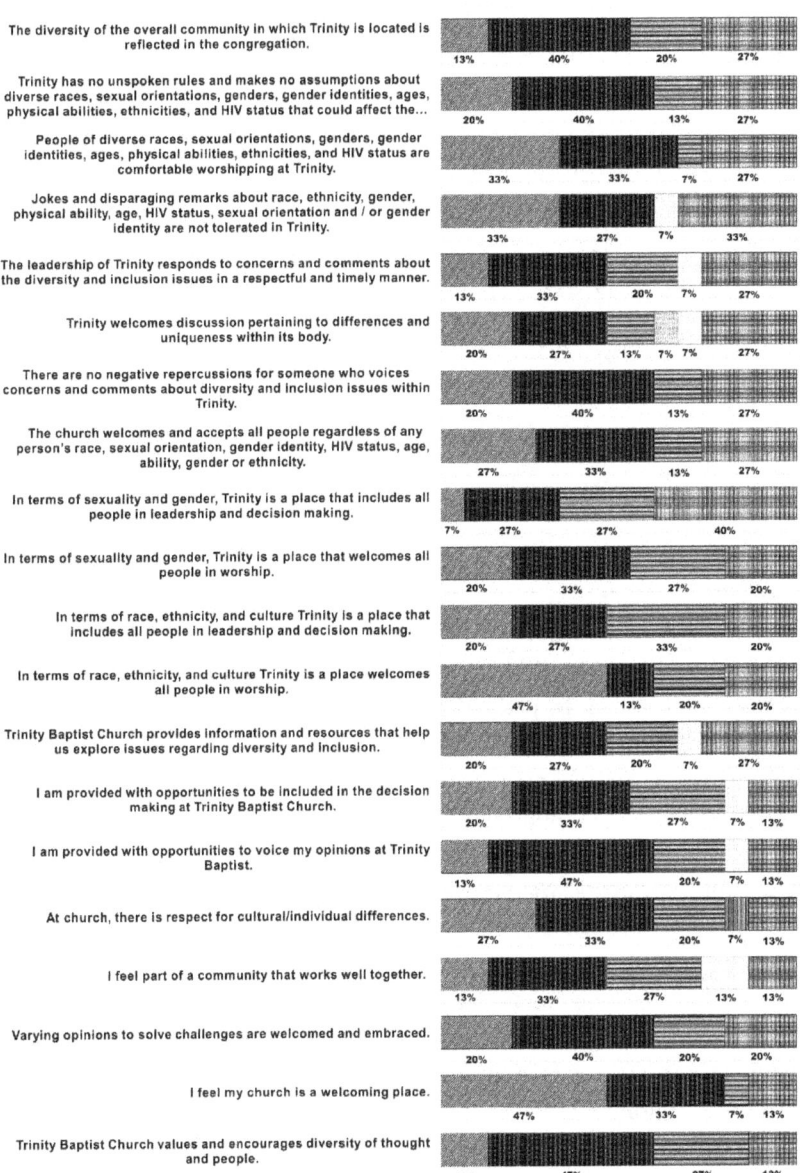

Figure 12. Initial Assessment of Diversity and Inclusion.

the participants began to talk about some of the young people whom they took into TBC to help. Eventually, they began to indicate that I was an example of an LGBTQ person they had accepted into TBC. The participants acknowledged that they "made space" for me so that I could do my ministerial project. The participants recognized that they needed to move beyond the DADT culture to one of transparency. They mentioned how some young people who seek authentic relationships have stopped coming to TBC without explanation. One participant provided greater detail on this in a one-on-one interview.

The groups were then asked to reflect on three final questions:

1. How can TBC become more authentic concerning issues of sexuality in the church?
2. How have these sessions contributed to your thoughts about being inclusive of those in "nontraditional" relationships or lifestyles?
3. How will you, in your role at TBC, advocate for inclusion at TBC?

The groups acknowledged that they needed to be themselves and avoid being pretentious. The participants, as a body, asked questions about what steps they could take to appear more authentic to others. I communicated that TBC would need to take extraordinary steps to exceed the stereotype of being homophobic because of their Afro-Caribbean heritage. The participants responded that they learned to be more careful with their words toward others and to be patient with newcomers. They acknowledged that the sermons caused them to think about their personal roles in extending hospitality to others. Moreover, some participants acknowledged that there is a struggle between faith and love when it comes to accepting LGBTQ persons. Several participants used the opportunity to declare that they had family members who were part of the LGBTQ community. For the first time, the participants were comfortable discussing their acceptance of those family members. They discussed how society has changed and how the conversation has shifted to public discourse about LGBTQ issues. When asked if they were comfortable advocating for LGBTQ persons at TBC, the participants acknowledged that they were. To sum up, one of the participants indicated that "everyone needs a church," and thus, they would be open to including everyone who came through their doors.

The session ended with Pastor Bembry telling the participants that there would be a discussion on the next steps for the development of RICH at TBC. However, he noted that the leadership of TBC wanted to know if I would

Ministry Implementation, Analysis, and Evaluation

continue to work with the congregation past the ministerial project. I indicated that if TBC was comfortable with the openness of my sexual identity and that my husband would also be welcomed, then I would continue to conduct ministry at TBC. The participants acknowledged that all would be welcome, especially my partner and me. Then the audience applauded.

The group was given a final assessment to complete. The participants consisted of one male and nine females who were laity, the executive leaders, worship leaders, and the pastor. All participants identified as over fifty-four years of age. The final survey was comprised of six questions using a similar scale of Strongly Agree, Agree, Disagree, Strongly Disagree, and Not Applicable. Overall, the participants responded with an average of 74 percent Strongly Agreeing with the statements about TBC using inclusive language to embrace all people, advocating on their behalf, becoming more welcoming and inclusive of LGBTQ persons, and individually welcoming others. The balance of an average of 22 percent Agreed with the statements (figure 13).

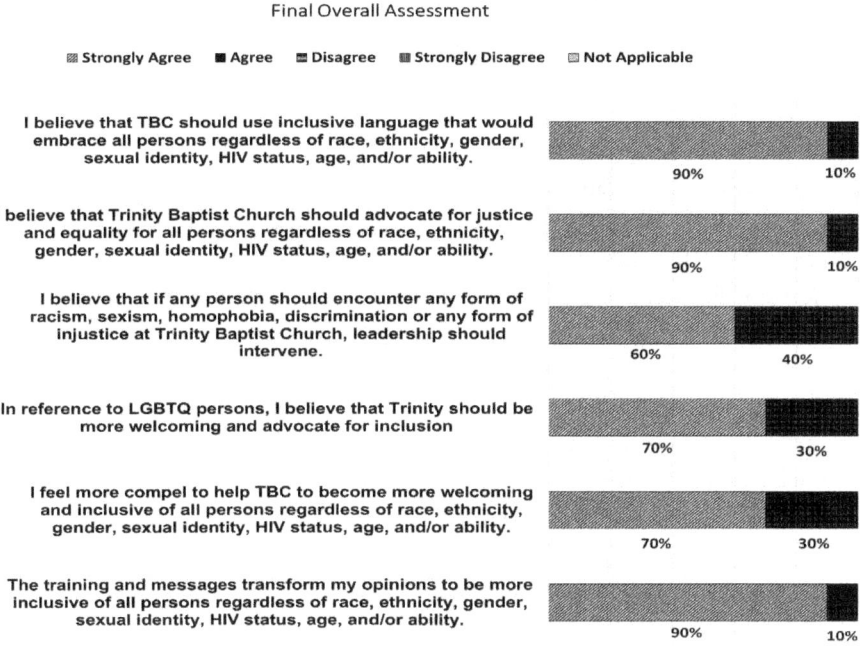

Figure 13. Results From Final Assessment Questionnaire

Ministry Data Evaluation and Assessment

The data from the Initial Assessment Questionnaires and Sermon Evaluation Questionnaires revealed that the participants felt that TBC should be welcoming toward LGBTQ persons. No one directly disagreed with the statements of hospitality through the data. However, the skipping of some of the questions by a small percentage gave me concerns. As evidenced by their responses to this concern in the discussion groups, there may be some who are still struggling with the matter and are, therefore, uncomfortable disclosing their true thoughts. Furthermore, the data demonstrated that a small percentage of the participants struggled with the statements of advocacy for LGBTQ persons and the inclusion of HIV persons. Although they felt that TBC should be welcoming, the issue of advocacy may have caused tension with the DADT culture. Furthermore, the issue of excluding HIV persons in leadership highlighted the stigma of HIV in the Black Church. These small percentages of dissent revealed further need for education about advocacy for others and dispelling the stigma of HIV. This could be done through more transformative preaching.

The interviews revealed that the DADT culture at TBC has contributed to an atmosphere of fear and secrecy. In spite of the "open-closet" practice of TBC allowing members of the LGBTQ community to participate in some of the ministries, LGBTQ persons may have departed because of the lack of affirmation and validation from TBC. Although many at TBC thought that simply having LGBTQ persons in their midst meant that TBC was an accepting congregation, the code of DADT created a space of unspoken hostility. Furthermore, the lack of advocacy for LGBTQ persons empowered the dissenters to control the presence of LGBTQ persons within TBC.

Through preaching on RICH as a gay minister, I facilitated the transformation of the DADT culture at TBC. Although I never spoke of my sexuality in the sermons and workshops until the final closing interview, the hearers of the RICH sermons felt empowered to break the DADT code and engage in authentic conversations about LGBTQ issues. TBC learned that silence about LGBTQ persons did not translate into genuine hospitality. Regardless of race, gender, sexual identity and/or orientation, all people want to be seen, heard, and included. The majority of the participants' willingness to advocate for LGBTQ persons was manifested, as many advocated for me behind closed doors. This will be discussed in the final chapter.

5

Summary, Conclusion, and Reflection

Summary and Conclusion

THROUGHOUT HISTORY, CHRISTIANITY HAS benefited from the various gifts of those who were rumored to have been a part of the queer community. Renaissance Europe had Leonardo da Vinci, Michelangelo, and King James. The Black Church and the Black community benefited from the activism of James Baldwin, Bayard Rustin, and Shirley Chisholm. Gospel music legend James Cleveland's songs have been published in the hymnals of multiple denominations. As churches continue to exploit the gifts of LGBTQ persons in the pews, without granting them access to power or permission to be their authentic queer selves, the church continues to perpetuate the cycle of oppression. Pastors, preachers, and lay leaders should observe that now that marriage equality has empowered LGBTQ persons to walk in the light, they will no longer tolerate sitting in the shadows of the Black Church being invalidated by heterosexism.

As I reconciled the data from the RICH surveys, the one-on-one interviews, and group discussions, it became evident that some of the key leaders of TBC were open and willing to extend inclusive, Christian hospitality to members of the LGBTQ community. In fact, some of them thought that they were already inclusive but did not recognize that the DADT culture of TBC oppressed LGBTQ persons. The stories of the LGBTQ people who left

TBC seem to support this. The DADT culture of TBC left many LGBTQ persons powerless against the dissenters that they encountered at TBC. Because no one advocated for them at the decision-making table and they did not advocate for themselves, TBC continued to perpetuate an atmosphere of homophobia. After the discussions about previous LGBTQ people being welcomed at TBC, the pastor of TBC disclosed to me that those who left did so because they did not want to cause conflict at TBC by living their "authentic" lives out in the open. Confrontation was avoided.

Yet, transformation requires direct confrontation. Martin Luther confronted the Catholic Church by nailing a copy of his ninety-five theses to the door of Wittenberg Castle. Rosa Parks confronted segregation by defiantly refusing to give up her seat on a Montgomery, Alabama, bus. The Reverend Dr. Martin L. King Jr. and other Civil Rights activists marched in defiant confrontation against police officers and pro-segregationists. The rioters at the Stonewall Inn stood in direct confrontation against New York City police who attempted to drag them to jail. Transformation begins with confrontation. Too often, preachers and pastors are either too complicit or too comfortable with the privileges of social affluence that they are afraid to have confrontation for fear of loss. Transformational preaching about inclusivity cannot proceed through heteronormativity, where there is a desire for diversity without discomfort.

With this said, the preacher must recognize her/his oppression within society or else she/he will not comprehend the nature of liberation necessary in preaching to diverse audiences. Homiletician Sarah Travis, in her essay "Troubled Gospel: Postcolonial Preaching for the Colonized, Colonizer, and Everyone in Between," stated, "Most preachers in the West are both perpetrators of imperial projects and simultaneously oppressed by these very systems."[1] The cultural and socioeconomic status of particularly Black heterosexual clergy from which they benefit often serves as an impediment to transformational proselytization. All preachers, regardless of their cultural background, may forget that they operate in a bubble or sphere of privilege, which may cause them to seem disconnected from the material realities affecting their hearers. James Nieman and Thomas Rogers, in *Preaching to Every Pew*, cautioned the preacher to be self-aware:

> Despite the erosion of public esteem that some say ministry has suffered, pastors continue to operate in a sphere of social privilege. Due to professional identity and education (and sometimes

---

1. Travis, "Troubled Gospel," 47.

income), they typically benefit in the overall scheme of class. Even when one's own personal background has been of a lower class, the simple fact of holding pastoral office relocates an individual and reinforces new ways of thinking and acting. As a result, preachers often easily lose touch with how to speak beyond this professionally achieved social location.[2]

Therefore, it may be easy for them to oversimplify the problem and misunderstand the situation, both in its causes and its cures.[3] The call to transformational preaching involves recognizing the need for the gospel's liberation in one's life, to discover in what ways he/she is oppressed, and to learn about how the same system which oppresses others also oppresses the seemingly powerful. The majority of the RICH ministry's participants recognized that in order to fulfill the "whosoever" biblical mandate of TBC,[4] they need to welcome and include LGBTQ persons in the full life of their church. As one of the participants stated during the final discussion, "Everyone needs a church, and we need them."

Reflection

It was Communion Sunday at TBC. The praise team was leading the congregation in a version of Sinach's "I Know Who I Am." It was an important Sunday because TBC was receiving into its fellowship two newly baptized believers, as well as two persons by way of Christian experience. I was one of those being received under watch care. It had been five months since I came down the church aisle seeking fellowship with TBC. And finally, after much debate among the deacon and deaconess boards, the privilege of membership has been extended to me. Feedback from the pastor of TBC to me indicated that although the boards voted to grant me membership, one person voted no. It was the same person who attempted to derail the RICH ministry by outing me to the rest of the boards. Yet, the leaders proceeded without his consent. This would be the first time at TBC that an openly gay man, as well as an ordained minister, would be granted the full rights and privileges of every member in the congregation. For a Baptist congregation, this was a major step, as indicated in Barnes's journal article

---

2. Nieman and Rogers, *Preaching to Every Pew*, 1190.

3. Travis, "Troubled Gospel," 55.

4. Revelation 22:17 is often paraphrased when the invitation to discipleship is extended to nonmembers during the Black Church worship experience.

R.I.C.H. in Preaching

"To Welcome or Affirm: Black Clergy Views About Homosexuality, Inclusivity, and Church Leadership." TBC's decision to extend membership, as well as leadership privileges, to an openly gay ordained preacher breaks the "hierarchy of tolerance characterized by inclusivity in membership but not leadership where the most coveted church positions are off-limits to openly gays and lesbians."[5] This ministerial project began with the proposal that transformational preaching could move perceived homophobic congregations toward a spirit of radical, inclusive Christian hospitality that embraces the LGBTQ community. It would seem that the data collected and action taken by TBC support that hypothesis.

The transformation of some of TBC's key strategic leaders' attitudes was a result of the embodiment of the preached Word about TBC being a RICH congregation. The embodiment occurred in three ways. First, the messages themselves were focused on evoking and empowering the hearers to love and embrace others regardless of their various identities. The messages drew upon a liberation theology of love, justice, and equality for all persons.

Second, the fact that the messages were proclaimed through an openly gay Black preacher while facing a few dissenters may have emboldened some who attended RICH to speak about their own experiences with members of the LGBTQ community. In addition, it should be noted that during this ministerial project, my mother accompanied me to Sunday worship services. Since the pastor of TBC had a previous pastoral relationship with my family, his role in promoting this ministry to the leadership team was advantageous. The pastor observed that the presence of my mother sent a message of parental affirmation and support that others within TBC witnessed. That action itself helped me preach the embodied Word of RICH.

Finally, my preaching empowered the participants to share their own experiences about family and friends in the LGBTQ community. Through transformational preaching, participants in RICH felt liberated to discuss with me their stories because of my personification of RICH. In other words, they found an ally. Having advocates and allies within the Black Church strengthens the bond of inclusion for LGBTQ people. The messages in RICH took on a new incarnation because I was liberated from some of the Protestant traditions that perpetuate the demonization and devaluation of the queer community and my own sexuality. The multisensory use of visuals through PowerPoint, in conjunction with my high tenor voice

---

5. Barnes, "To Welcome or Affirm," 1424.

Summary, Conclusion, and Reflection

and androgynous gestures, served to enhance communication. Sally Brown and Luke Powery, in *Ways of the Word: Learning to Preach for Your Time and Place*, wrote:

> People hear and see sermons. Onlookers may see that the Lord is good based on how one uses one's body in preaching. Preaching then is not just word but also deed. It is active and action. The body speaks and may say some things that verbal speech cannot articulate. The body is the core of human communication. The word event, preaching, is an embodied event. There has to be somebody present to preach, and Christian bodies are temples of the Spirit, graced with the potential to sound and body forth human experience of the divine. Preachers are stewards of the holy in and through the body. Thus, great care should be given to our bodies in preaching.[6]

In essence, comfort with preaching about RICH requires authenticity. Preachers must be comfortable within their own skin and physique, acknowledging the privileges or lack thereof that may accompany them.

Therein may lie some of the problems with the Black Church. The fear of advocating for LGBTQ persons often brings the stigma of being gay-by-association. The issue with many Black churches is that many have not been conditioned to address the hard discussions on sexuality without relying on traditional fundamental stances of abstinence and heterosexism. The sermons during the RICH training enabled participants to become comfortable with expressing their views through the intentional practice of liberating love. The participants of RICH were liberated to feel safe about their struggles and/or comfort with LBGTQ persons in their affinity circles and community by the preached Word. The fear of being scrutinized by other peers within the church seemed to vanish as they began to indicate that they had family, friends, and coworkers who were members of the LGBTQ community. More specifically, the pastor received a "wake-up" call regarding his own congregants. This process allowed some TBC leaders to confess to him previously unheard "family secrets" of LGBTQ members. His own perception of his congregation being homophobic was transformed.

Through preaching, TBC has moved beyond their former DADT and tolerance of LGBTQ persons toward loving people for who they are. Pastors and people in the Black Church should know that having LGBTQ people in music ministries, on worship teams, and on usher boards while

---

6. Brown and Powery, *Ways of the Word*, 103.

maintaining a culture of DADT does not make them inclusive churches. DADT in the Black Church does not create a space of acceptance and love; rather, it controls the involvement of LGBTQ people. Tolerance as a means of maintaining church financial viability through the contributions of LGBTQ persons to the Black Church experience—music, worship, prayer, call-and-response—is oppressive exploitation.

Advocates for LGBTQ persons are needed. More pastors, preachers, and lay leaders should serve as allies for those without a voice or representation at the decision-making table. The Reverend Kenneth Samuel, in the article "Taking a Lead on Faith: Four Black Pastors at the Forefront of LGBT Equality," said, "As preachers, we have to echo a message of inclusivity of all people in the family of God."[7] In the same article, the Reverend Jacqui Lewis added, "If the pastor speaks a prophetic word about LGBT inclusion, even if they're first met with resistance, it can begin to change the hearts and minds of our community."[8] Such was the transformation of the participants of RICH at TBC.

Reflection on the penultimate question posed to me by some of the key leaders participating in RICH captured the transformation. This question was posed: "Reverend Torrence, are you going to stick around after this research?" It was accompanied by a comment:

> Since you were seeking watch care, the main reason we haven't moved forward with giving you the right hand of fellowship was because we weren't certain if you would still be here after your project.[9]

The question was revelatory. In spite of the holdout vote by one participant, the others were concerned about my intention to continue at TBC. After making it clear that I would not uphold DADT and that my husband would need to be welcomed, as well, I stated, "So, if you are saying that you are making room for me to do ministry at TBC as my authentic self, then we can talk."[10] The group responded with a "yes." Transformation had taken place. That transformation was getting the strategic leaders of TBC to talk about the proverbial elephant in the room. It seemed that they were waiting for someone to break the DADT culture of TBC. Through hearing

---

7. McLeod, "Taking a Lead on Faith," para. 2.
8. McLeod, "Taking a Lead on Faith," para. 4.
9. Participant from final group discussion and interview.
10. Final group discussion and interview.

Summary, Conclusion, and Reflection

sermons about RICH, the participants were empowered to break through their DADT wall of silence.

Next Steps toward LGBTQ Inclusivity

When the leaders of TBC asked their final question—What actions could be taken to be perceived as more inclusive?—that demonstrated their care and concern for being hospitable to LGBTQ persons. The challenge for TBC and other churches like it will be to surpass the general stereotype that Afro-Caribbean churches are homophobic. I recommended taking radical steps; such as either posting visible signage (rainbow emblem) in front of the building welcoming LGBTQ persons or making a general statement every Sunday that clearly welcomes LGBTQ people. Whether or not TBC will take these actions is unknown. However, the pastor and leaders of TBC wanted me to continue the efforts toward making the congregation a RICH church. Toward this end, the RICH workshops will continue in the form of a RICH ministry.

As TBC strives toward LGBTQ inclusion, further Bible studies on the subjects of sexuality, equality, and justice will need to occur. These studies should increase the dialogue about LGBTQ persons in the kingdom of God. The research in this ministerial project also revealed the need for support ministries for family members and friends of LGBTQ people in TBC, such as a discussion and/or prayer group.

TBC has been very active in the Brooklyn community with a variety of outreach ministries. If it is to become inclusive of LGBTQ people, then it must also address and advocate for some of their issues. Collaborative efforts with organizations such as the Brooklyn Community Pride Center (BCPC) will help TBC tap into some of the issues facing the LGBTQ community. Having some of the volunteers of BCPC conduct informative seminars will contribute to this endeavor.

Within the Baptist denomination, there are entities advocating for LGBTQ inclusion. Rainbowbaptists.org provides a directory of resources as well as a listing of welcoming and affirming Baptist congregations around the nation. Similarly, Gaychurch.org is an online directory for LGBTQ persons seeking gay welcoming congregations. As TBC begins to become more inclusive, it would benefit from being listed on such internet sites. Finally, the Association of Welcoming and Affirming Baptists (AWAB) is the only organization dedicated to establishing welcoming and affirming worship spaces within the Baptist tradition. Along with providing a toolkit, AWAB can serve as a resource for TBC as it becomes more inclusive.

This ministry has laid a foundation for TBC to open its doors to the LGBTQ community. As I continue to work with the pastor and leadership of the church, more dialogue about diversity and inclusion will occur. The sad reality of the church is that many assume that the church knows what it really means to be hospitable to others regardless of race, gender, age, sexual identity, and various abilities. If this assumption were true, many of our churches would be diverse. Radical, inclusive Christian hospitality recognizes this false assumption and challenges the church to emulate the radical and inclusive love of Christ. TBC has begun the process of transformation toward emulating the love of Christ by having an openly gay, ordained minister on the leadership team and at the decision-making table. That is a step in the correct direction in the ongoing transformation process toward becoming a RICH church.

Appendix A

Strategic Planning Initial Assessment Questionnaire

Name of the Church: _____

Date: _____

1. How frequently do you attend Trinity church?

    ☐ 1–2 times per month ☐ 3–5 times per month
    ☐ Once every 2 months ☐ Other
    ☐ Do not wish to disclose

2. How would you describe your role at TBC? (Check ALL that apply)

    ☐ Church member ☐ Minister/clergy
    ☐ Executive leadership board/council
    ☐ Worship leadership ☐ Standing subcommittee member
    ☐ Do not wish to disclose

3. What gender are you?

    ☐ Male ☐ Female ☐ Do not wish to disclose

4. Sexuality Identity:

    ☐ Heterosexual ☐ LGBTQIA ☐ Do not wish to disclose

Appendix A

5. Which age group do you belong to?

   ☐ 17 or under ☐ 18–25 ☐ 25–38 ☐ 39–53
   ☐ 54–72 ☐ 73 or older ☐ Do not wish to disclose

6. How do you racially/ethnical identify? (Check all that apply)

   ☐ Black/African American ☐ Caribbean American
   ☐ LatinX/Hispanic American
   ☐ Asian/Pacific Islander American
   ☐ Indian/Middle eastern/Arab American
   ☐ White/Anglo American ☐ Bi-/Multiracial American
   ☐ Non-American Citizenship

7. In reference to the following statements, please place an X in the boxes that apply below.

	White/Anglo/Caucasian American	African/Caribbean American	LatinX/Hispanic American	Asian/Pacific Islander American	Christian	Non-Christian	LGBTQ (Gay/Trans)	Other
I have *family* members who identified as	☐	☐	☐	☐	☐	☐	☐	☐
I have *friends* who identified as	☐	☐	☐	☐	☐	☐	☐	☐
I have *neighbors* who identified	☐	☐	☐	☐	☐	☐	☐	☐
I have *coworkers* who identified	☐	☐	☐	☐	☐	☐	☐	☐

Strategic Planning Initial Assessment Questionnaire

Based on the above how likely are you to invite the following to worship at Trinity Baptist Church?

*Please circle a number at the end of each statement.	Not likely	Maybe if changes were implemented	Likely	Most Likely
White/Anglo/Caucasian family members, friends, coworkers, and/or neighbors	1	2	3	4
African/ Caribbean American family members, friends, coworkers, and/or neighbors	1	2	3	4
LatinX/ Hispanic family members, friends, coworkers, and/or neighbors	1	2	3	4
Asian/Pacific Islander family members, friends, coworkers, and/or neighbors	1	2	3	4
Christian family members, friends, coworkers, and/or neighbors	1	2	3	4
Non-Christian family members, friends, coworkers, and/or neighbors	1	2	3	4
LGBTQ (Gay/Trans) family members, friends, coworkers, and/or neighbors	1	2	3	4

Appendix A

Based on your experience, how do you feel that the following persons are treated at Trinity Baptist Church?

	Treated equally	Treated less favorable	Treated more favorable
Men	☐	☐	☐
Women	☐	☐	☐
African/Caribbean/Black American Persons	☐	☐	☐
White/Caucasian/Anglo	☐	☐	☐
LatinX/Spanish/Hispanic Persons	☐	☐	☐
Asian/Pacific Islander Persons	☐	☐	☐
Indian/Middle Eastern/Arab Persons	☐	☐	☐
Native-American/ Indigenous Persons	☐	☐	☐
LGBTQ Persons	☐	☐	☐
Youth/Teens/ Children	☐	☐	☐
The Elderly/Senior Citizens	☐	☐	☐
Divorced Persons	☐	☐	☐
Widows/Single Persons	☐	☐	☐
Non-English-Speaking Persons	☐	☐	☐

Strategic Planning Initial Assessment Questionnaire

	Treated equally	Treated less favorable	Treated more favorable
Persons with Questionable Immigration Status	☐	☐	☐
Physical Disabled Persons	☐	☐	☐
Persons with College Experience	☐	☐	☐
Person with No College Experience	☐	☐	☐
Persons with Low or No Income	☐	☐	☐
Persons with High Income	☐	☐	☐

In your opinion, how do you feel that the following persons should be treated at Trinity Baptist Church?

	Treated equally	Treated less favorable	Treated more favorable
Men	☐	☐	☐
Women	☐	☐	☐
African/Caribbean/Black American Persons	☐	☐	☐
White/Caucasian/Anglo	☐	☐	☐
LatinX/Spanish/Hispanic Persons	☐	☐	☐
Asian/Pacific Islander Persons	☐	☐	☐

Appendix A

	Treated equally	Treated less favorable	Treated more favorable
Indian/Middle Eastern Persons	☐	☐	☐
Native American/Indigenous Persons	☐	☐	☐
LGBTQ Persons	☐	☐	☐
Youth/Teens/Children	☐	☐	☐
The Elderly/Senior Citizens	☐	☐	☐
Divorced Persons	☐	☐	☐
Widows/Single Persons	☐	☐	☐
Non-English-Speaking Persons	☐	☐	☐
Persons with Questionable Immigration Status	☐	☐	☐
Physical Disabled Persons	☐	☐	☐
Persons with College Experience	☐	☐	☐
Person with No College Experience	☐	☐	☐
Persons with Low or No Income	☐	☐	☐
Persons with High Income	☐	☐	☐

Strategic Planning Initial Assessment Questionnaire

*Please circle a number at the end of each statement.	Strongly Agree	Agree	Disagree	Strongly Disagree	N/A
In terms of race, ethnicity, and culture Trinity is a place welcomes all people in worship.	1	2	3	4	5
In terms of race, ethnicity, and culture Trinity is a place that includes all people in leadership and decision making.	1	2	3	4	5
In terms of sexuality and gender, Trinity is a place that welcomes all people in worship.	1	2	3	4	5
In terms of sexuality and gender, Trinity is a place that includes all people in leadership and decision making.	1	2	3	4	5
The church welcomes and accepts all people regardless of any person's race, sexual orientation, gender identity, HIV status, age, ability, gender or ethnicity.	1	2	3	4	5
There are no negative repercussions for someone who voices concerns and comments about diversity and inclusion issues within Trinity.	1	2	3	4	5
Trinity welcomes discussion pertaining to differences and uniqueness within its body.	1	2	3	4	5

Appendix A

*Please circle a number at the end of each statement.	Strongly Agree	Agree	Disagree	Strongly Disagree	N/A
The leadership of Trinity responds to concerns and comments about the diversity and inclusion issues in a respectful and timely manner.	1	2	3	4	5
Jokes and disparaging remarks about race, ethnicity, gender, physical ability, age, HIV status, sexual orientation and / or gender identity are not tolerated in Trinity.	1	2	3	4	5
People of diverse races, sexual orientations, genders, gender identities, ages, physical abilities, ethnicities, and HIV status are comfortable worshipping at Trinity.	1	2	3	4	5
Trinity has no unspoken rules and makes no assumptions about diverse races, sexual orientations, genders, gender identities, ages, physical abilities, ethnicities, and HIV status that could affect the worship environment.	1	2	3	4	5
The diversity of the overall community in which Trinity is located is reflected in the congregation.	1	2	3	4	5

Strategic Planning Initial Assessment Questionnaire

*Please circle a number at the end of each statement.	Strongly Agree	Agree	Disagree	Strongly Disagree	N/A
Trinity Baptist Church values and encourages diversity of thought and people.	1	2	3	4	5
I feel my church is a welcoming place.	1	2	3	4	5
Varying opinions to solve challenges are welcomed and embraced.	1	2	3	4	5
I feel part of a community that works well together.	1	2	3	4	5
At church, there is respect for cultural/individual differences.	1	2	3	4	5
I am provided with opportunities to voice my opinions at Trinity Baptist.	1	2	3	4	5
I am provided with opportunities to be included in the decision making at Trinity Baptist Church.	1	2	3	4	5
Trinity Baptist Church provides information and resources that help us explore issues regarding diversity and inclusion.	1	2	3	4	5

Appendix B

Strategic Planning Participant Feedback Form

Name of the Church: _____
Date: _____
Message Title: _____
Scripture Reference: _____
Preacher/Presenter: _____

Your feedback is important! We care about what you carry home from today's lesson(s), so your reaction to the questions below will help us ensure that you are well spiritually transformed and empowered.

Based on the Sermon Presentation please circle a number at the end of each statement.

	Strongly Agree	Agree	Disagree	Strongly Disagree	N/A
Overall the message was faithful to the scripture.	1	2	3	4	5
I understood the main point of the message.	1	2	3	4	5

Strategic Planning Participant Feedback Form

	Strongly Agree	Agree	Disagree	Strongly Disagree	N/A
The message engaged my mind.	1	2	3	4	5
The introduction got my attention.	1	2	3	4	5
The introduction laid the foundation for the message.	1	2	3	4	5
The message had a clear outline.	1	2	3	4	5
The message had momentum.	1	2	3	4	5
The main message was unified	1	2	3	4	5
The illustrations edified the message.	1	2	3	4	5
The transitions were clear.	1	2	3	4	5
The message length was appropriate.	1	2	3	4	5
The language and vocabulary were understandable.	1	2	3	4	5
The preacher made good eye contact.	1	2	3	4	5
The message spoke to my areas of interest.	1	2	3	4	5
The message sparked an interest to learn more.	1	2	3	4	5

Appendix B

As a result of hearing the message:

	Strongly Agree	Agree	Disagree	Strongly Disagree	N/A
Trinity should be welcoming to all people regardless of race.	1	2	3	4	5
Trinity should be welcoming to all people regardless of sexual orientation.	1	2	3	4	5
Trinity should be welcoming to all people regardless of gender identity.	1	2	3	4	5
Trinity should be welcoming to all people regardless of HIV status.	1	2	3	4	5
Trinity should be welcoming to all people regardless of age and ability.	1	2	3	4	5

Based on the Sermon Presentation please circle a number at the end of each statement.

	Strongly Agree	Agree	Disagree	Strongly Disagree	N/A
I believe that Trinity should offer opportunities for all persons to participate in the ministries/committees/leadership of the church regardless of race.	1	2	3	4	5
I believe that Trinity should offer opportunities for all persons to participate in the ministries/committees/leadership of the church regardless of sexual orientation.	1	2	3	4	5

Strategic Planning Participant Feedback Form

	Strongly Agree	Agree	Disagree	Strongly Disagree	N/A
I believe that Trinity should offer opportunities for all persons to participate in the ministries/committees/ leadership of the church regardless of race gender identity.	1	2	3	4	5
I believe that Trinity should offer opportunities for all persons to participate in the ministries/committees/leadership of the church regardless of race HIV status.	1	2	3	4	5
I believe that Trinity should offer opportunities for all persons to participate in the ministries/committees/ leadership of the church regardless of race age and/or physical ability.	1	2	3	4	5

As a result of hearing the message:

	Strongly Agree	Agree	Disagree	Strongly Disagree	N/A
I would advocate for the inclusion of all persons to be welcomed at Trinity regardless of race.	1	2	3	4	5
I would advocate for the inclusion of all persons to be welcomed at Trinity regardless of immigration status.	1	2	3	4	5

Appendix B

	Strongly Agree	**Agree**	**Disagree**	**Strongly Disagree**	**N/A**
I would advocate for the inclusion of all persons to be welcomed at Trinity regardless of sexual orientation.	1	2	3	4	5
I would advocate for the inclusion of all persons to be welcomed at Trinity regardless of gender identity.	1	2	3	4	5
I would advocate for the inclusion of all persons to be welcomed at Trinity regardless of HIV status.	1	2	3	4	5
I would advocate for the inclusion of all persons to be welcomed at Trinity regardless of age and ability.	1	2	3	4	5

Appendix C

Strategic Planning Final Assessment Form

Name of the Church: _____

Date: _____

1. How would you describe your role at TBC? (Check ALL that apply)
   - ☐ Church Member   ☐ Minister/Clergy
   - ☐ Executive Leadership Board/Council
   - ☐ Worship Leadership   ☐ Standing Subcommittee member
   - ☐ Do Not Wish to Disclose

2. What gender are you?
   - ☐ Male   ☐ Female   ☐ Do Not Wish to Disclose

3. Sexuality Identity?
   - ☐ Heterosexual   ☐ LGBTQIA   ☐ Do Not Wish to Disclose

4. Which age group do you belong to?
   - ☐ 17 or Under   ☐ 18–25   ☐ 25–38   ☐ 39–53
   - ☐ 54–72   ☐ 73 or Older   ☐ Do Not Wish to Disclose

Appendix C

5. How do you racially/ethnical identify? (Check all that apply)

☐ Black/African American ☐ Caribbean American
☐ LatinX/Hispanic American
☐ Asian/Pacific Islander American
☐ Indian/Middle eastern/Arab American
☐ White/Anglo American ☐ Bi-/Multiracial American
☐ Non-American Citizenship

After attending the trainings in Radical Inclusive Christian Hospitality, I believe that . . .

*Please circle a number at the end of each statement.	Strongly Agree	Agree	Disagree	Strongly Disagree	N/A
The training and messages transform my opinions to be *more* inclusive of all persons regardless of race, ethnicity, gender, sexual identity, HIV status, age, and/or ability.	1	2	3	4	5
I feel *more* compel to help TBC to become more welcoming and inclusive of all persons regardless of race, ethnicity, gender, sexual identity, HIV status, age, and/or ability.	1	2	3	4	5
In reference to LGBTQ persons, I believe that Trinity should be more welcoming and advocate for inclusion	1	2	3	4	5
I believe that if any person should encounter any form of racism, sexism, homophobia, discrimination or any form of injustice at Trinity Baptist Church, leadership should intervene.	1	2	3	4	5

Strategic Planning Final Assessment Form

*Please circle a number at the end of each statement.	Strongly Agree	Agree	Disagree	Strongly Disagree	N/A
I believe that Trinity Baptist Church should advocate for justice and equality for all persons regardless of race, ethnicity, gender, sexual identity, HIV status, age, and/or ability.	1	2	3	4	5
I believe that TBC should use inclusive language that would embrace all persons regardless of race, ethnicity, gender, sexual identity, HIV status, age, and/or ability.	1	2	3	4	5

Appendix D

Sermon

A Vision to Rise Up

Scripture: Acts 10:9-23, 34-35 (NRSV)

NELSON MANDELA ONCE STATED that "action without vision is only passing time, vision without action is merely daydreaming but vision with action can change the world."[1] Are you a community just passing time with special programs and social gatherings? Are you a people with great ideas but no follow-through to make those ideas into reality? Or are you a church that puts the vision into action by actively pursuing the vision? For transformation to occur in our lives, our churches, and communities, we need visionaries who are not afraid to act and persons of action who are great visionaries. John Maxwell indicates that vision is the ability to see (awareness), the faith to believe (attitude) and the courage to do (action)[2]. So, for us, we need those who are aware, those with attitude, and those who are not afraid to act—a diversity of talent to get to the preferred future we need. Simply because I am one who truly believes that the future just doesn't happen; it is influenced by visionary leaders. The future is a cumulative product of the hard labor put forth by people of vision. It is a dream birthed into reality. The progress that many of us are enjoying today is a combination of the efforts made by people of vision several

---

1. This quote is widely attributed to Nelson Mandela, though the original source cannot be located.
2. Maxwell, *21 Most Powerful Minutes*.

decades ago. People like Henry Ford—who thought of mass-producing automobiles; Benjamin Spock—who influenced child-rearing among baby boomers; John Dewey—father of educational reform in America; Ray Kroc—responsible for franchising McDonalds; activists—Susan B. Anthony, Gandhi, Marcus Garvey, Malcolm X, and Martin Luther King, Harvey Milk—were visionaries. Steve Jobs, the founder of Apple Computers, iPad, and iPhone, etc., was a visionary leader.

Lovett Weems says that a vision "catches us up, captivates, and compels us to act. It is the gift of eyes of faith to see the invisible, to think the unthinkable, and to experience the not yet."[3] It is a sign of things hoped for, yet unseen. A vision keeps a community going. And to keep the church going, its people need a vision for "where's there is no vision, the people perish" (Prov 29:18).

George Barna defines a vision as a "clear and precise mental portrait of a preferable future, imparted by God to His chosen servants, based on an accurate understanding of God, self, and circumstances."[4] To understand the vision, one must have an understanding of God, self, and circumstances. Here is where we see the struggle of the Apostle Peter. God sends him a vision, but he struggles to understand God, the circumstances and himself.

He has a relationship with God, but he is still struggling to understand. Peter always struggled with understanding God. Although he understood Jesus to be the son of God and made a public declaration of faith to that fact, he struggled with the notion that Jesus would have to die on the cross, which caused Jesus to say, "Satan get thee behind me." Peter struggled to keep his focus on Jesus as he tried to walk on water, but he almost drowned. There was a struggle when Jesus fell to his knees to wash Peter's feet. Peter initially said no, until Jesus told him, unless I wash you, you will have no part of me. Peter struggled with the notion that he would deny knowing Christ three times, and even though he promised Jesus. He not only denied knowing Jesus but curse his accuser before realizing hearing the cock crow three times. He would even struggle to understand what it meant to love Jesus. When Jesus asked him three times, "Simon, Peter, do you love (*agape*) me more than these; meaning will you sacrifice your life for me?" Peter could only respond, "Jesus, you know I love (*philos*) you; meaning, I love you like a brother." So, Peter always struggled in his relationship with getting to understand the Lord better.

3. Weems, *Church Leadership*, 6.
4. Wells, "Vision and Mission," para 5.

Appendix D

This incident upon the roof is no different. We are told that Peter was on his rooftop praying, got hungry and fell into a trance. He gets a vision of a white sheet being filled with all these unclean creatures of the earth and is told by God three times to rise, kill and eat, and three times Peter says no. The story says that he woke up puzzled, lacking the understanding of what God was trying to communicate to him.

Here is where we note some critical observations. First, a vision will come when you are available and accessible to God through prayer, and you have a hunger for God's will—doing the work of the kingdom. This is where Peter was in his life. His heart sought after the things of God. Blessed are they which do hunger and thirst after righteousness for they will be filled (Matt 5:6). Seek ye first the kingdom and all its righteousness, then these things will be added unto you (Matt 6:33). Real ministry and true worship will make you hungry to do the will of the Lord. A relationship with God will give you an appetite to see those kingdoms of this world become the kingdom of our Lord. And to various degrees, we are all somewhat spiritually hungry. Some here are hungry to see the unsaved people in their own homes saved. Others are hungry to see our church pews filled, and the church budget met. Others are hungry to see various ministries and activities revitalized. The church is filled with hungry people and when you are hungry there is a tendency to get grouchy and "hangry." There is a tendency to snap at people and to tell them off because you are hungry. So, you have to forgive us occasionally if you see us biting each at other. It is only because we are spiritually hungry.

Secondly, although the vision may be clear, the methods of achieving it may be somewhat murky. In fact, it will take faith. The vision for Peter was clear: rise, kill and eat. The challenge for Peter was to gain understanding about performing the task when the very practice went against his cultural framework. This is where we see his struggle with the circumstances and self. The circumstances: Peter has been taught about the various prohibitions and abominations that were deemed uncleaned throughout the Old Testament, especially in Leviticus. Yet he has this vision to eat all these animals, reptiles, birds, and creeping things (as the King James Version describes it). In modern times, these would include our pulled pork sandwiches, smoked hams, fried pork chops, shellfish (crabs and lobsters), escargot (snails), deep-fried catfish, conch, frog legs, and calamari (squid). But these dietary prohibitions would be synonymous with the other prohibitions considered to be uncleaned or excluded from the temple of worship:

the uncircumcised, eunuchs, lepers, women on their menstruation, body tattoos and piercings, same-sex relationships, touching dead bodies, wearing mixed fabrics, lying, stealing, adultery, and being unwelcoming to foreigners. It's all unclean behavior. So, what should one do when the vision of God contradicts your cultural norms and religious understanding?

For Peter, God uses his physical hunger to communicate the keys to satisfying his spiritual hunger because the food of the spiritual man and woman is to know and to do God's will. Peter has a rooftop vision, but his basement mentality is keeping him from understanding it.

Have you ever been hungry and get at the dinner table to only get disappointed at what was being served? You may turn up your noses at the plate of ham hocks when you really had a taste for steak. There is a tendency in the church to turn up our noses at the souls that God wants to bring into the church; souls that will satisfy our spiritual hunger. These are the things in our society that we don't really want to take in. Like Peter trying to understand the vision on the rooftop, we must confront the items in our basement. We have a rooftop vision but a basement mentality. What's in your basement that you are struggling with?

- The drug addict or those struggling with addiction—they are welcome here, but we will not allow them to host an NA meeting.
- The baby's mama with different fathers for each of her children.
- Or the father with different baby mamas.
- The ex-con still out on probation trying to get his life together; yet, when folks find out, he was in jail.
- The immigrant with undocumented status seeking assistance.
- The unmarried couple who been living together for years.
- The members of the LGBTQ community who are good enough to be in your music ministry but not good enough to join couples consulting or to have their kids be a part of your children church/Sunday school.

For many within the church, there are things in our society that many don't want crawling and creeping into the church. Yet God is giving us the opportunity to satisfy our hunger and be reminded that there was a time, they many did not want any of you in the church and used biblical scripture to validate their stance.

Appendix D

Radical inclusive Christian hospitality (RICH) begins with our willingness to do as Peter did. He was to rise, kill, and eat. We are to rise, resist, and receive.

Rise: being willing to go beyond our perceptions and our understanding of others. Increase your cultural IQ. Peter's cultural IQ is tested. He isn't familiar with non-Jewish dietary habits or customs. He knows how to be a Jew; but a Gentile, not so much. Rise by increasing our circle of friends. Peter does just that when God sends him three strangers, and he invited them into his home. Like Abraham, who invited the three strangers into his home, Peter uses that same spirit of hospitality.

Then kill: We must confront our biases. And when we are talking about inclusive ministry, we have to clean out our basement mentality. Peter's biases are being revealed: implicit and unconscious. What is bias? Bias is a prejudice in favor of or against one thing, person, or group compared with another, usually in a way that's considered to be unfair. Biases may be held by an individual, group, or institution and can have negative or positive consequences. There is conscious bias (also known as explicit bias) and Unconscious bias (also known as implicit bias). There are not just limited to ethnicity and race but can include a person's age, gender, gender identity, physical abilities, religion, sexual orientation, weight, and many other characteristics.

Unconscious biases are social stereotypes about certain groups of people that individuals may form outside their own conscious awareness. We all hold unconscious beliefs about various social and identity groups, and these biases stem from one's tendency to organize social worlds by categorizing. Especially when we find ourselves in situations of high stress, and in need of self-protection and preservation, we make quick assessments about those around us by trying to place them into neat boxes of "friend or foe." So, for a quick frame of reference, we tend to use that which we've heard through personal experiences about others who are different from us. These frames of references usually are based on a skewed perspective of what we have seen of the worst and/or best of people in other cultures. For instance, we may have a bias against other African Americans as untrustworthy, lazy, or incompetent, which is why we often don't do business with our own people. Biases—the blacker the berry, the sweeter the juice. Biases—black attitude. Those are the biases against our own kind. For others, it may be that Jews are the best lawyers—they know how to argue and negotiate. We may think it's a compliment, but it is a stereotype. All Asians are good at mathematics and the sciences. Then there are those biases which are insults: Latinos do not speak English well; they bring down property values when they move into a neighborhood because they bring in their entire clan; Arabs and Indians are Islamic terrorists and hostile to women; lesbians are super masculine; gays are extremely feminine; young people are not dependable and selfish.

And when we think like that, it demonstrates that we have all lost the proper frame of reference in which to view our neighbor. When Jesus views us, the Lord does not look through tinted lenses coated with biases. And although we are all falling short of the glory of God, Jesus still views us with compassion and love. So, in order to understand God's vision, you have to confront those issues within yourself that keep you from seeing others as the Lord sees them. Listen to God's rebuke of Peter's statement, "I have never eaten anything that is profane or unclean." God responds: "What God has made clean; you must not call profane." Through the salvific gift of Christ, God has made clean a lot of things we consider profane. We should resist and destroy those stereotypes to which we hold on. Kill off the bigotry, hatred, and love our neighbors as we love ourselves.

Finally, eat. Receive others into our communities and lives. Take them in. Peter not only invited strangers into his home, but he establishes a relationship and follows them to their community. He learns that he has more in common with them than that which is different. They all wanted a closer relationship with God. And when we are talking about inclusive ministry, we have to clean out our basement mentality. To get to the point of clarity of God's vision whereby we too can say like Peter, "I truly understand that God shows no partiality, but in every nation, anyone who fears him and does what is right is acceptable to him." Inclusive ministry means being able to put on the mind of Christ and being transformed as Romans 12:2 urges us to become, and walking in the shoes of Christ as we embrace all of God's children regardless of their background, identities, imperfections, etc. Amen.

APPENDIX E

Sermon

Who Is My Neighbor?

Note: A video clip of Mr. Rogers singing "Won't You Be My Neighbor?" is shown prior the sermon

Scripture: Luke 10:25-37

MANY MAY BE SURPRISED to know that Mr. Rogers was an ordained Presbyterian minister. For young audiences, this minister attempted the address the question "who is my neighbor," causing young minds to examine levels of compassion, and hospitality. It is a question that we should ask ourselves as we strive to become a radical, inclusive Christian ministry. For Trinity Baptist Church, "Who is my neighbor?"

And that is a relevant question, considering that the community of Crown Heights is changing. According to the US Census Bureau, as of July 2017, Brooklyn had a 5.8 percent increase in its population. In Crown Heights, Central Brooklyn, the population has grown to 292,870 persons. The median age of the current population is thirty-three years old. The marital status of this population has only 54,860 people being married, and over twice as much—138,982 being single. The ethnic composite consists of 77 percent white, 11 percent Hispanic or Latino, 9 percent African American, 5 percent Asian, and 3 percent other. Twenty-five years ago, it was a neighborhood sieged by racial tension between blacks and Hasidic Jews,

Sermon

with street riots and gun violence. Now it is ground zero for gentrification, with median rents of $2,000 for a one-bedroom apartment and people protesting for the humane rights of chickens. The good news of gentrification is that the neighborhood has become more attractive to people with higher levels of income. This, in turn, has diversified the community population as well as breaking down bubbles of cultures. The bad news is that individuals with lower incomes are being displaced. Familiar mom-and-pop shops are closing and becoming organic and gourmet shops. The neighborhood has changed and still is changing.

So, the challenge for Trinity as it sits in the midst of this neighborhood with a newly constructed apartment building in its backyard is not only to know who my neighbor is but to do as Jesus commanded and love the neighbor as ourselves. In the midst of change, God's people are challenged to still reach the lost beyond their cultural normative. Evangelism through radical, inclusive Christian hospitality is key. The commission to go and make disciples of all nations, baptizing them in the name of the Father and of the Son and of the Holy Spirit, takes on new meaning, especially when the nations have moved into your backyard. So, for us, this is an opportunity to explore the possible levels of evangelism.

The legendary missionary strategist Ralph D. Winters surmises that there are four levels of evangelism: E-0, E-1, E-2, and E-3.[1]

E-0 Evangelism is evangelism that takes place within the church. This is reaching out to those who already attend or participate in local church activities. Examples of this kind of evangelism in local church practice would be Sunday school evangelism, Christmas musicals, homecoming, and perhaps follow-up visitation. There is no need for the Christian to move outside of his own culture or cultural boundary, as the one he is seeking to reach is already a part of it. Its greatest focus is renewing wayward Christians and bringing those who participate but haven't yet believed to the point of a personal decision.

E-1 Evangelism is evangelism that takes place outside of the church but to the same culture. This is reaching out to those who do not participate in any local church activities, but otherwise, have mostly similarities with respect to cultural views and practices. A good example of this in local church practice is personal evangelism (invite a friend Sunday). There is very little need for the Christian to move outside of his own culture, as the one he is seeking will already fit in pretty well with the church culture. Its greatest

---

1. Winter and Koch, "Finishing the Task," 15.

focus is on reaching lost family members of Christians, their coworkers, and others with whom they may already associate outside of the church.

E-2 Evangelism is cross-cultural evangelism into a similar but different culture. This is reaching out to those who may or may not speak the same language but certainly, have different backgrounds. The best example of this in local church practice is probably "door to door ministries, outreach programs, and church-sponsored short-term mission trips to other countries" (Lott Carey). Here there is a need for the Christian to stretch himself and become aware of his own cultures' additions to biblical practices, as the one he is seeking will often find them to be hindrances to faith. Its greatest focus is not on bringing people into the church but rather bringing the church to a new place.

E-3 Evangelism is cross-cultural evangelism that takes the message of Christ to cultures very different from that of the messenger. This is reaching out to those who have never heard of Jesus or who have a culturally instated resistance to Christianity. There are usually no examples of this in local church practice, except in the commissioning of career missionaries.

Here, there is a need for the Christian to radically strip off his own culture from the gospel message and identify the barriers, gaps, and bridges to the faith that exist in the unreached person's culture. Its focus is exclusively on bringing the church to a new place.

One mode of confronting gentrification is for the church to extend itself to level E-2 and E-3 evangelism. And for RICH (radical, inclusive Christian hospitality), this means going beyond our affinity groups to reach others of varying cultural backgrounds. For the Christian, the neighbor may not be of your similar culture, religion, race, creed, sex, gender, and/or sexual orientation. This is the lesson that Jesus gives to us, in Luke 10, as Jesus answers the question "Who is my neighbor?"

For the Jew in this context, the neighbor was defined as "one who was near" or a fellow Jew. The one, who is like me, thinks like me and looks like me. Yet, in the parable of the Good Samaritan, Jesus gives a story of a nameless person. We only know that he was a "man." We do not know his religion, race, creed, sexuality, moral value, political belief, social class and/or status. We only know that he was attacked, robbed, beaten and left for dead. This is the crime scene.

The road to Jericho was also known as the "bloody way." It wasn't unusual to hear of such events such as robberies, murders, rapes, and various crimes. Much like Crown Heights and other parts of Brooklyn in the '80s

Sermon

and '90s, the road had a violent reputation. And although the neighborhood is improving, there are still modes of violence. Hate crimes against Jews and members of the LGBT community are still prevalent, as well as individuals calling the police on people for being Black; yet in the wrong place. Racial tensions are still high as communities are being financially robbed by large corporate building projects. We are living in a microcosm of society's turmoil: mass shootings, xenophobia, and closed borders.

And as society witnesses these atrocities, there are various responses. Jesus tells us in this story of the Samaritan that all parties involved saw the victim:

There are the violators. These are those who saw him as an opportunity for theft and possible murder. For them, this person was a means to an end. Like, the senior citizen on his/her way to the market or bank is being beaten and mugged; the teenager being shot in the head for their brand-new Jordans and expensive coating on their way to/from school. Or the driver in their expensive vehicle being carjacked. There are violators who spot potential victims daily. They see opportunities to express hate against those who are different from the norm. The neo-Nazi who sees Jews and Blacks as a threat to their whiteness. The nationalist who sees Mexicans and Muslims as a threat to their safety and security. And the religious right who sees feminists and LGBT persons as a threat to their patriarchal hierarchy. There are violators who see potential victims every day.

Then there are the voyeurs. Jesus says that after this man was victimized, a priest and Levite saw him, but they cross to the other side. The priest represents the organized religion—the church hierarchy who often get so busy with performing their duties within the church that they will not help those outside the church. Biblically the priests in the Jewish tradition performed the sacred rites of the people. In order to do so, they needed to remain clean. So, a priest seeing a "potential" dead thing like this man lying on the side of the road would try to avoid touching it or being touch by it. It would have interrupted his service to the temple. The Levite represented the "community" of the Jewish nation, which was instructed to avoid contamination from such things as well. So, both the church and the community avoid the victim because he was "unclean." It's a shame when both the church and the community turn away from the helpless. Jesus beckons us to respond as the Samaritan being valiant.

The valiant are the ones willing to take a chance by showing mercy through *their approach, association, attention, assistance,* and *assignment.*

Appendix E

Approach: The difference between the valiant Samaritan and the voyeurs is their willingness to approach and offer hospitality. The word translated "mercy" has its origins in a Hebrew word *chesed*, which means "the ability to get right inside the other person, to see with his eyes, to think with his thoughts, to feel with his feelings." It involves empathy, sympathy, and compassion. The Samaritan cared enough to not only display empathy and sympathy but compassion. In order to reach others, we must extend compassion. Too often, as "churchgoers," we are just comfortable with displaying empathy: feeling the same emotions as the other person or displaying sympathy where we feel sorrow or concern for the other person. Compassion requires us to feel care and warmth for the other person. We must approach others with compassion. You can't win souls to Christ, acting like Rambo. People are already hurting emotionally, spiritually, and physically. So, our approach must be one of compassion. This is the essence of hospitality.

Association: The Priest and Levite feared contamination. Many of us may fear contamination through association. What will others think about me if I associate myself with this person? If I associated with the members of the LGBTQ community, will people start to question my own sexuality? It's a fear of contamination through association. Some of us are so conscious of our image that we limit our circle of friends to those who make us look good. But thank God for Jesus, who was not ashamed to be accused of being "a glutton and a drunkard, a friend of tax collectors and sinners!" (Luke 7:34).

Attention: The Samaritan cares for this person—caring for his wounds by pouring oil and wine then bandages them. Those who come into our midst need care irrespective of race or religion. This is hospitality. Many are hurt; furthermore, they are suffering from "church hurt," which is a bad or traumatic encounter with organized religion and/or its participants.

Assistance: Reaching means extending ourselves beyond our comfort zones, schedules, and cultural norms to take the stranger into our lives. Henri Nouwen defines hospitality "as primarily the creation of free space where the stranger can enter and become a friend instead of an enemy. Hospitality is not to change people, but to offer them space where change can take place." The word hospitality can be traced back to the Hebrew/Aramaic word *hachnasat orchim*, which literally translates to the bringing in of strangers. This is what Jesus refers to in Matthew 25:35–36: "For I was hungry and you gave me food, I was thirsty and you gave me something to

Sermon

drink, I was a stranger and you welcomed me, I was naked and you gave me clothing, I was sick and you took care of me, I was in prison and you visited me."

Assignment: Finally, there is the assignment to the innkeeper. "Take care of him; and when I come back, I will repay you whatever more you spend." The reality is that only Jesus saves. We do not. However, as the body of Christ, we have the charge of the innkeeper to care for those whom Jesus brings to our doors. We may not be able to take the risk of the Samaritan who sacrificed time, talent, and finances, but we can function effectively and collectively as the innkeeper.

Jesus will supply us the means to care for them. The Samaritan supplied the innkeeper with the finances to care for this man while he recovers with a promise to repay what is owed.

Jesus will repay what we sow into the lives of others. Do not be deceived; God is not mocked, for you reap whatever you sow (Gal 6:7). I may not be able to be the Samaritan, but I can, at minimum, be the innkeeper. For the church, there is a twofold charge. First, go and do likewise as the Samaritan. We do this through outreach ministries and evangelism. And secondly, be good innkeepers for those who are placed in our care. Here is where many need improvements. We can get them in church, but what do you do after they are here?

Appendix F

Sermon

Radical, Inclusive, Christian Hospitality in Worship

Scripture: Revelation 7:9–17

MARTIN LUTHER KING JR. once said 11 a.m. Sunday is the most segregated hour in America.[1] Now, almost sixty years later, eight in ten American congregants still attend services at a place where a single racial or ethnic group comprises at least 80 percent of the congregation, while one in five may worship in a congregation where no single racial or ethnic group predominates. According to the Pew Research Center (PRC), a majority (57 percent) of congregants overall are part of congregations that are predominantly (at least 80 percent) non-Hispanic white. Additionally, 14 percent of Americans who attend services do so at houses of worship with a membership that is at least 80 percent black (including 5 percent who are in congregations that are entirely black). And another 8 percent attend churches where at least eight in ten churchgoers are Hispanic.[2]

Yet, the challenge for most traditional churches is diversity and inclusion. The Reverend Lovett H. Weems Jr., the director of the Lewis Center for Church Leadership at Wesley Theological Seminary in Washington, DC, says that

> the nation is getting younger and more diverse and the church is getting older and less diverse. . . . There is an increasing gap

---

1. King, "Most Segregated Hour."
2. Lipka, "Many U.S. Congregations," para 6.

Sermon

between the makeup of the church and the people God has given us in the United States to minister with.[3]

In fact, the majority of traditional houses of faith are still the least diverse in America. PRC shows that the most diverse faith practices are the Seventh-day Adventists, Muslims, Jehovah's Witnesses, and Buddhists.[4]

The fact of life is that God has placed us in a world of diversity. Desmond Tutu says that

> we inhabit a universe that is characterized by diversity. God created us as a diverse people in a diverse world. And His love for variety is not just visible in us but in all aspects of His creation. Look at the many species in any ecosystem all living in synchrony, or the changing seasons, each allowing for growth and harvest. God wants unity for God's people which is why he gave us different skills and strengths so that we would recognize our need for one another and appreciate our individuality.[5]

But in our world, our differences are often used as a means to create distance between us. A hatred for diversity doesn't reflect a love for the One who created it. Author Audre Lorde says that "it is not our differences that divide us. It is our inability to recognize, accept, and celebrate those differences."[6] What separates us is hate. Love unites. "Those who say, 'I love God,' and hate their brothers or sisters are liars; for those who do not love a brother or sister whom they have seen, cannot love God whom they have not seen" (1 John 4:20).

In the church, we generally hold one of three perspectives concerning diversity. First, they are those who hold the "melting" pot concept for diversity, whereby we all lose our unique cultural identities and take on the predominant culture around us. So, when people join this church, they need to adapt to us and not us adapt to them. When it comes to worship, many of us still prefer to worship with others who look like us, think like us, and act like us. We want the new people coming into our doors to like our music, like the Bible verses we like, like the ministries we support, and, finally, like us.

---

3. Hahn, "Ethnic Diversity," para 4.
4. Lipka, "Diverse U.S. religious groups," para 6.
5. Tutu, "Our Glorious Diversity," para 1.
6. This quote is widely attributed to Audre Lorde, though the original source cannot be located.

Appendix F

Next, there are those who may say we should be like a "salad bowl," whereby our cultural differences are appreciated while we are integrated into the broader community. We coexist. We tolerate each other and accommodate each other's differences, but we do not learn from each other. And as with any salad, there is still a tendency for similar items to cling together—creating cliques and fractions. But we do function together for the greater cause. Then there is the kaleidoscope perspective, where both the people and the larger society adapt and change. It is a mosaic of all the uniqueness within its boundaries. When we are talking about the diversity and inclusion in the body of Christ, we are envisioning the beautiful mosaic of God's people. A kaleidoscope perspective allows us to celebrate each person's differences because of their beauty, usefulness, and because they are the work of the hands of our Lord in heaven.

Discipleship is not about duplication or assimilation, but it is about emulation of the love of Christ in his followers so that there can be the utilization of the diversity of their talents in the kingdom. Bishop Desmond Tutu observed, "Isn't it amazing that we are all made in God's image, and yet there is so much diversity among his people."

In the Revelation of John, the exiled apostle has a vision of a multitude of people that emulated the kaleidoscope of humanity. He sees this vision because, according to the New American Bible Revised Edition, he is caught up in the spirit on the Lord's Day (Rev 1:10). He is an outcast, yet he is still in the spirit. In spite of the troubles and tribulations around him, he is still in the spirit. So often, many of us allow our circumstances to dictate our spiritual aptitude and attitude toward God. Many cannot see the vision for the church because they are caught up in everything else but the Spirit. We cannot grasp what God has destined for us because we get caught up with the busyness of life. Caught up with schedules and deadlines. Caught up with our love lives or our loveless life. Caught up with the chaos of politics. Caught up with the latest tweeter feed and/or Facebook post. Caught up with the busyness of church—the struggles of the church finances, the power struggles between the boards and committees, and the power struggles between the pulpit and the pew.

Many of us can't see the vision because we get caught up in everything else but the Spirit of God. And they that seek to worship God, must worship the Lord in spirit and in truth. We would be so much further in our pursuit of the vision God has for us if we would just grasp the God of the church we go to, rather than the church of the God we worship.

Sermon

God and God's kingdom are so much larger than a building. And this is what is being revealed to the Apostle John when he says, "After this, I looked, and there was a great multitude that no one could count, from every nation, from all tribes and peoples and languages, standing before the throne and before the Lamb, robed in white, with palm branches in their hands."

The first thing that he notices is the diversity of the worshippers. Worship in heaven is diverse and inclusive of God's people. The countless multitude that is gathered before the throne of God is made up of worshipers from "*all tribes and peoples and languages.*" And really this should not be a surprise because Jesus told the temple merchants that "my house shall be called a house of prayer for all the nations" (Mark 11:17). We are reminded that all are invited to respond to the grace of God and join in worship, and none should be prevented. All people are created in the image of God and discover their true worth in the worship of God. The church is made strong, and its witness made real when worship is inclusive.

John hears various languages as this worship occurs. So, this diversity is not just about representation and tokenism. It recognizes the cultural differences of the participants. For the most part, many of our worship services are monocultural based on a Western-Christianized template. For the most part, all is done in one predominant language and style. So, to be inclusive, like John, we should be able to hear the "languages of the many people" around us. Therefore, our worship should reflect the cultural differences of the attendees, which in itself builds community.

Our worship should be inclusive because of the promise of salvation to those who are willing to believe. They cried out in a loud voice, saying, "Salvation belongs to our God who is seated on the throne, and to the Lamb!" Inclusive worship should demonstrate that Salvation is available to all. It's an individual choice, but salvation is still available to all. 1 John 1:9: "If we confess our sins, he is faithful and just, and will forgive our sins and cleanse us from all unrighteousness."

Coretta Scott King once said, "I still hear people say that I should not be talking about the rights of lesbian, and gay people and I should stick to the issue of racial justice. But I hasten to remind them that Martin Luther King Jr. said, 'Injustice anywhere is a threat to justice everywhere.' I appeal to everyone who believes in Martin Luther King Jr.'s dream to make room at the table of brother and sisterhood for lesbian and gay people."[7]

---

7. King, "1996 Atlanta Gay Pride."

Appendix F

Salvation is a personal experience that is publicly confessed. Our salvation experiences are diverse. How we each have come to know Jesus is diverse. But redemption itself is inclusive. An elder explains to the writer of Revelation that the multitude is made up of persons who "have washed their robes and made them white in the blood of the Lamb. For this reason, they are before the throne of God, and worship him day and night." We worship because God has broken down every barrier that stands before us and divine righteousness and has given the gift of Jesus Christ so that we might stand in righteousness before the throne of God. One the deaconess quoted the fourth verse of the Solid Rock, saying, "When He shall come with trumpet sound, Oh, may I then in Him be found, Clothed in His righteousness alone, Faultless to stand before the throne! On Christ, the solid Rock, I stand; All other ground is sinking sand."

Humanity has been bought for a price, and that price was the precious blood of Jesus. John 3:16: "For God so loved the world that he gave his only Son, that whoever believes in him should not perish but have eternal life."

So, when we celebrate, we are not only commemorating the birth of Christ and when God's *Kairos* time intersected with our *Chrono's* time, but we celebrate the promise of Christ's return for his church—a diversity of persons. No one knows the day nor the hour, but whether it's during good times or evil times—we can count on his coming like a thief in the night. The millennial is looking for that church as well—the church that walks the talk as well as talks the walk. The church that stands for social justice reaches out for the outcasts in the community and advocates an inclusive community for all.

Appendix G

Sermon

Loving the Stranger in a Culture of Fear

Scripture: Deuteronomy 10:12-19

THERE IS A BELIZEAN saying, "*Blood tika dan wata but wata tase betta. Blood is thicker than water but water taste better.*" Meaning: sometimes, interacting with friends or strangers is less stressful than interacting with problematic or difficult relatives. The older I get, the more I tend to believe the accuracy of that proverb, especially after a holiday season of being around family. Yet, we live in a world where we were taught to "beware" of the stranger. As a latchkey kid growing up in the inner city, it was stated to me often to keep the windows and doors locked; stay clear of strangers; don't talk to strange people; and, don't enter strange places. This may be why many of us, who have been taught similar lessons, protect our homes with dogs and double locks, our buildings with vigilant doormen, our roads with anti-hitchhike signs, our subways with security guards, our airports with safety officials, and our cities with armed police and our country with an omnipresent military. Although we might want to show sympathy for the poor, the lonely, the homeless, and the rejected, our feelings toward a stranger knocking on our door and asking for food and shelter are ambivalent at the least.

When we think about the nine victims at the Emanuel African Methodist Episcopal Church, who allowed a stranger, a young white man, to enter into their Bible study and prayer space, we are reminded how their

Appendix G

hospitality was met with the worst form of hostility. They were massacred. So, the evil in our world incites us to fear our neighbors and the stranger. The stranger: Latin migrant caravans beckoning at our southern borders; hooded young teenagers walking down the block; fellow airline passengers who seem hyper or dressed in Muslim outfits. The stranger: people who are unfamiliar, speak another language, have a different skin color, wear different types of clothes, have different sexual orientations, and gender identities, and/or live a lifestyle different from ours. They are the strangers who make us afraid and even hostile. Rosemary Joyce, professor of anthropology at UC Berkley, indicates that "xenophobia is an unreasonable fear or hatred of foreigners or strangers or of that which is foreign or strange."[1] It is interesting that for people of faith, fear seems to dictate our motives for excluding strangers. It is a fear that if too many of those strange people come into our worship place, we will no longer recognize it as ours. Fear that we may lose control and become powerless in an environment where we once had some clout. Why? Because in general, we have been trained to have a hostile attitude toward the unknown. In our world, the assumption is that the stranger is a potential danger, and it is up to them to disprove it. They are strangers being estranged from our culture and commands, our levels of sensibilities, and our comfort zones.

As a result, we become guarded and suspicious. We are careful with our behavior—what we do and say around them—after all, we don't know them well enough to truly be ourselves. We don't allow them into our reality to see who we truly are. That is a hostile attitude. For example, when Jesus asked the Samaritan woman at the well for water, her initial response was one of suspicion. As Christians, we are even leery of each other. We suspect the preacher. We don't quite trust the deacon. We are suspect of the treasurers and trustees. And if we can't trust those who we kneel at the altar with every week and call sister and brother, then how could we possibly trust strangers. The truth of the matter is that we, as believers, need to learn how to receive each other first before we can work on receiving strangers. Think about it. If we don't trust, respect, and love the saints, then how can we extend a warm welcome to strangers? And I mean more than just saying with our lips, "Peace of the Lord be with you," but showing in our lives the peace of the Lord is with us, and we are extending that peace to others, as well. Being authentic in our welcome communicates that we are not threatened by others, but we are comfortable being around them and with them. And that

---

1. Joyce, "Fear of the Other," line 1.

is an action that requires us not just being cordial but being compassionate: not just greeting people with a hello and welcome but asking sincerely, "How are you? And what can I do to help you?" And the greatest lesson that every congregation must learn is how to become more hospitable to each other and outsiders. My belief is that one of the reasons there is a lack of participation in the various ministries and activities of the church is that the congregation has not effectively created a "safe place" for people to be just "themselves." No one will share their talents with the people who he/she fears. And it's a hard truth—a difficult truth and one that often hurts.

So how do we become more hospitable? How do we embody God's love for us by loving the stranger? And what is the benefit of loving the stranger?

For Moses and the people of Israel, hospitality is summarized in this command: You shall also love the stranger, for you were strangers in the land of Egypt. In Deuteronomy 10, as Moses tries to give the Israelites a second opportunity to keep God's commandments, he reminds them not only about the Ten Commandments but their obligation to the stranger in their midst. They are told to fear the Lord God, to walk in obedience to the Lord, to love the Lord, and to serve the Lord God with all their heart and soul. The evidence of this reverence, obedience, love, and service should be manifested in their treatment of each other and the stranger.

So, when we offer hospitality to others, we do it out of reverence for God, which is the fear of the lord. The philosopher Paul Woodruff once said,

> Reverence is the virtue that keeps people from trying to act like gods. To forget that you are only human, to think you can act like a god—this is the opposite of reverence. Reverence is the recognition of something greater than the self—something that is beyond human creation or control that transcends full human understanding.[2]

An irreverent soul who is unable to feel awe in the presence of things higher than the self is also unable to feel respect in the presence of things it sees as lower than the self." For instance, we cannot claim to revere and love God while simultaneously declaring that certain portions of our neighbors are evil. We should be able to see portions of God in each other. No wonder when the Day of Judgment occurs, Jesus says we will be judged based upon how we treated each other. Jesus tells us that on the Day of Judgement, all nations will be separated like a herder separates his sheep from the goats with sheep on the right and goats on the left. "Then He will say to those

---

2. Woodruff, *Reverence*, 3.

on his right, 'Come, you who are blessed by my Father; take your inheritance, the kingdom prepared for you since the creation of the world. For I was hungry, and you gave me something to eat, I was thirsty, and you gave me something to drink, I was a stranger, and you invited me in, I needed clothes, and you clothed me, I was sick, and you looked after me, I was in prison, and you came to visit me.' Then the righteous will answer him, 'Lord, when did we see you hungry, thirsty or a stranger or in prison or sick?' The Lord will reply, 'Truly I tell you, whatever you did for one of the least of these brothers and sisters of mine, you did for me.' Then he will say to those on his left, 'Depart from me, you who are cursed, into the eternal fire prepared for the devil and his angels. For I was hungry, and you gave me nothing to eat, I was thirsty, and you gave me nothing to drink, I was a stranger, and you did not invite me in, I needed clothes, and you did not clothe me, I was sick and in prison, and you did not look after me.' They also will answer, 'Lord, when did we see you hungry or thirsty or a stranger or needing clothes or sick or in prison, and did not help you?' He will reply, 'Truly I tell you, whatever you did not do for one of the least of these, you did not do for me.'" The writer Hebrews reminds us as well (13:2) do not forget to show hospitality to strangers, for by so doing, some people have shown hospitality to angels without knowing it.

When we offer hospitality, we offer it out of obedience to God's word. Besides Exodus, there are approximately twenty-five other biblical references that exert the call to care for strangers, particularly in Leviticus 19:33–34: "When a stranger resides with you in your land, you shall not do him wrong. The stranger who resides with you shall be to you as the native among you, and you shall love him as yourself, for you were aliens in the land of Egypt; I am the LORD your God." If we love Jesus, we will keep his commands. If we keep his commands, his love abides in us.

When we offer hospitality, we offer it out of love for God and his love for us. Loving and serving God as well as demonstrating that love and service to each other will reveal the servants of God. After all, John the Apostle reminded the early church, "Whoever claims to love God yet hates a brother or sister is a liar. For whoever does not love their brother and sister, whom they have seen, cannot love God, whom they have not seen. And he has given us this command: Anyone who loves God must also love their brother and sister" (1 John 4:20–21). To offer hospitality is to love others. In fact, the Greek word for hospitality, *philoxenos*, comes from two words: *philos*, meaning love, and *xenos*, meaning stranger. So, hospitality is the love of strangers.

When we offer hospitality, we offer it out of service. Letty Russell, in *God's Welcome in a World of Difference*, defines hospitality as "the practice of God's welcome, embodied in our actions as we reach across difference to participate with God in bringing justice and healing to our world in crisis."[3] Hospitality involves reaching, bringing justice, and healing. Arthur Sutherland, in *I Was a Stranger: A Christian Theology of Hospitality*, indicates that

> Christian hospitality is the intentional, responsible, and caring act of welcoming or visiting, in either public or private places, those who are strangers, enemies, or distressed, without regard for reciprocation.[4]

Finally, Henri Nouwen goes further and says that to understand what hospitality can mean, we must first become a stranger ourselves.[5]

Moses and the words of God in Deuteronomy 10 remind all of us in some form or another that we were once strangers, as well. Each one of us has a unique experience from the journey we have taken to get to where we are now. For Afro-Caribbean people, our ancestors were strangers in this new world of the Americas, coping with the strangeness of systemic enslavement based on race. Most of them were not immigrants, but they were human cattle, tricked and trapped, captured and conquered, shackled and shamed, bred and brought, used and abused. And when slavery was done, they were ostracized and oppressed, discriminated against and denied. We, too, were strangers in a land that did mistreat, abuse, and use us. Our own journey of oppression and abuse should serve as a catalyst for having empathy for others. And this is what Moses wanted the Israelites to remember, that those who were oppressed should not become oppressors to others. Now that you have the privilege of some political, social, economic, and financial power, do not use that power to exclude and mistreat the stranger. Because as the recipients of deferred dreams, broken glass ceilings, and generational prayers, we often forget that we too were once strangers dwelling in a strange land. As we witness Latin migrants being walled out at our nation's borders, children being separated from parents and placed in cages, and Muslims banned from entering our countries, we often forget

---

3. Russell, *Just Hospitality*, 20.
4. Sutherland, *I Was a Stranger*, 17.
5. Nouwen, *Reaching Out*, 19.

that the only entry for many of our ancestors was in the bows of slave ships. We often forget that their families were often separated upon arrival and placed in cages, chains, and shackles. So, as we hear this monologue from the lawgiver Moses to the Hebrews children, there is a moment of recall to never forget that in the land we dwell, we too were strangers. And yet, as we were regarded as objects of prejudice, discrimination, stereotypes, racism, and other microaggressions, God loved us through it. God took us in. We went through, but we were not alone. God was still with us.

As receivers of God's grace, we must, in turn, pass it on. This is the message that Moses tells the Israelites as he challenges them to be the people that God wants them to become. The first covenant they broke with the building of the golden calf. God is giving them a second chance. Moses comes to them with a second set of tablets that not only reminds them of loving God and serving him, but it will challenge them as they learn to love their neighbors as themselves. We learn that God is a forgiving God. Radical hospitality is forgiving. We know how this story ends. God would send his son as a stranger to these people. They would curse him, kill him, and cast him out; yet, during the process, Jesus would still declare, "Father, forgive them for they know not what they do." The challenge for us as we reach out in the spirit of radical hospitality is to be able to still invite others in who may use and abuse us. Standing in the shoes of Christ, we still must invite the stranger into our lives with a spirit of forgiveness. Let's think back to Mother Emmanuel AME. It is an example of a group of people taking in a stranger. And although the stranger slaughtered their loved ones, they embodied the God of love and forgave him.

The real question we should ask ourselves when it comes to hospitality is about our capacity to offer love, forgiveness, mercy, and compassion to others.

Appendix H

Sermon

Speaking Words of Hospitality

Scriptures: John 1:1–4, 14; and 1 John 1:1–3

PLEASE STAND UP AND remain standing if you have ever been the victim of name-calling because of your race, gender, sexuality, religion, and/or physical looks. Please stand up and remain standing if you have ever called someone a derogatory name because of their race, gender or sexuality, religion, and/or physical looks. Please stand up if you have ever been the subject of a rumor or gossip? Please stand up if you have ever repeated a rumor or gossip? Please stand up if anyone has ever been nice to you to your face then talked about you behind your back? Please stand up if you have ever been the victim of any negative conversation directed at you. Please stand up if you have ever shared your goals, aspirations, dreams, and ambitions with others and was told that you could not accomplish them. Thank you. You may be seated.

The fact of our reality is that many of us have been victims of other people's negative words, or we have violated others with our own. Our words and language can be used for good purposes or bad purposes. Words can build up or tear down; they can be used to create or destroy; words can heal, or they can harm. Words are powerful tools in creating human consciousness, building communities and giving a relational context for social resilience. Such was the case for the words written by Thomas Jefferson:

Appendix H

> We hold these truths to be self-evident, that all men are created equal, that they are endowed by their Creator with certain unalienable rights, that among these are life, liberty and the pursuit of happiness.[1]

Those words began a revolution and helped build a nation. Or, the words of Martin Luther King: "We will not be satisfied until justice rolls down like waters and righteousness like a mighty stream,"[2] which galvanized the civil rights movement. With the right words, our language can create new opportunities.

As ambassadors of Christ, each and every one of us is given opportunities to use our words as instruments of hospitality. We are presented with the chance to create a welcoming space so that others can enter and come to know the love of God. Hospitality involves giving of self in the form of words and actions. Through words, we speak our minds to others, giving up our privacy and inviting others to share in our thoughts. When we refuse to speak, we close ourselves off from others. Furthermore, when we speak ugly words, we empower the dark forces around us. So, we must be careful in how we use our words. This is what the notable author, activist, and scholar Maya Angelou states . . . (Show clip):

> Words are things. You must be careful, careful about calling people out of their names, using racial pejoratives and sexual pejoratives and all that ignorance. Don't do that. Someday we'll be able to measure the power of words. I think they are things. They get on the walls. They get in your wallpaper. They get in your rugs, in your upholstery, and your clothes, and finally into you.[3]

Maya Angelou simply says, "Don't do that," but the reality is that we often do. Our mouths tend to negate our witness to God. That which we say contradicts our actions.

Our words have power. And yes, the Lord knows our hearts, but our words can reveal what is in our hearts. That is what Jesus told his followers when he said, "What comes out of the mouth proceeds from the heart, and this is what defiles" (Matt 15:18). Therefore, if we are to be effective witnesses for Christ, as the early followers of Jesus in our text, who proclaim, "We have seen his glory," then our words should reflect that glory. If you

---

1. Jefferson, "Declaration of Independence," para 2.
2. LeTourneau, "Until Justice Rolls Down," para 4.
3. Angelou, "Power of Words."

love me, then choose your words wisely. Don't tell me that you love me and then call me out my name. Don't tell me that you are showing me the love of God, then call me the n-word because of the color of my skin, or the b-word, because of my gender, or the f-word because of my sexuality. Choose your words carefully.

And although many of us believe that we are good and moral human beings who do not consciously practice racism, sexism, classism, and homophobia or embrace bigotry and various forms of prejudices, we still may unconsciously practice various forms of microaggressions because of how we speak to others. A microaggression is an everyday exchange that sends denigrating messages to others because of their race, gender, sexual identity, religion, and so on. It may simply be manifested as a microinsult by using terms like "CP time" or saying to a Jamaican, "How many jobs you got, man?" because those colloquiums perpetuate stereotypes about certain groups of people. It could be a microinvalidation which occurs when we ignore the presence of others by not recognizing their culture, gender, and sexual identity. We pretend that they do not exist and have nothing worth contributing: like making general statements about the godly family being a husband, wife, and children, which sends the message to single-parent families or same-sex families that they are ungodly and/or abnormal. Or you could just be bold and consciously degrade others with a microassault like Kevin Hart jokingly did when he talked about killing his son if he found out he was gay. Or President Number 45 calling nations like Haiti, Nigeria, and other African places s–hole countries.

We have to choose our words carefully. One of the problems of our current society is that we have lost the capacity and wisdom of thoughtful discourse. We have been ushered into a world of speaking the first thoughts that come to our minds. Our tongues are out of control. It was true then, and it is true now that "no one can tame the tongue—a restless evil, full of deadly poison. With it, we bless the Lord and Father, and with it, we curse those who are made in the likeness of God."

And whether we know it or not, it is my belief that regardless of your denomination, most so-called Christians speak in tongues every day. Regardless of how you feel about the gifts of the Holy Spirit, many of us *can* speak and *do* speak in tongues.

We speak with lying tongues, as the writer of Proverbs 25:18 says, "Bearing false witness against our neighbors." We speak with flattering tongues as indicated by the writer of Psalms 12, giving fake compliments

Appendix H

and building up other people. Or we are building up ourselves speaking with proud tongues, being boastful and full of ourselves while refusing to listen to others because we think we know it all.

For some of us, our tongues are overused, causing us to sound foolish. This is what the writer of Ecclesiastes 5:3 means when he says that "a fool's voice is known by multitude of words." Some people sin by simply overusing their tongue because they think they appear smart by doing a lot of talking, but the scriptures tell us just the opposite. God doesn't like a blabbermouth.

Some of our tongues are too swift, as it says in Proverbs 18:13, giving an answer before we have heard everything. That's why we are cautioned to be swift to hear and slow to speak.

Some of us have a backbiting tongue, sowing discord in our social networks. Scriptures tell us to beware of the backbiters. The elders used to say to beware of a dog that brings you a bone because he will always take one back with him.

The backbiters are often kindred spirits with those of a gossiping tongue. Leviticus 19:16 says, "Thou shalt not go up and down as a talebearer among thy people." And although some of us are good at quoting Leviticus against the LGBTQ community, when it comes to gossiping, we get silent.

Some of us are working with a cursing tongue and don't know that with every curse, we are closing ourselves off from being blessed by God. "As he loved cursing, so let it come unto him: as he delighted not in blessing, so let it be far from him. As he clothed himself with cursing like as with his garment, so let it come into his bowels like water, and like oil into his bones" (Ps 109:17–18).

And even though we may not be people who curse, we may still have a piercing tongue, which means that we tend to talk to others with sharp words and/or a nasty tone. Proverbs 12:18 speaks of this tongue when it says the words of reckless pierces like a sword. We have to watch our tone with others.

And some may be guilty of having a silent tongue and not speaking up because of our faith. Jesus said, "Whosoever, therefore, shall be ashamed of me and of my words in this adulterous and sinful generation; of him also shall the Son of man be ashamed when he cometh in the glory of his Father with the holy angels" (Mark 8:38). If we are not guilty about not speaking up for Jesus, then we may be guilty of not speaking up for justice. Leviticus 5:1: "When any of you sin in that you have heard a public adjuration to

Sermon

testify and—though able to testify as one who has seen or learned of the matter—do not speak up, you are subject to punishment."

Be it Pentecostal, Baptist, Catholic, Episcopalian, Presbyterian, or whatever denomination, many so-called Christians are speaking in a variety of tongues. The church has gotten a bad reputation of being a place where its members offer smiles of hospitality while their mouths stink with hostility. No wonder people are avoiding our churches because the so-called people of God are suffering from spiritual bad breath. But the good news is that God has a solution. There isn't a diagnosis for which God lacks a remedy. For our spiritual halitosis and gingivitis, God has something stronger than Listerine. That solution is the Word of life, Jesus.

Jesus is what the writer of John introduces his community to as it struggles to find common ground in a chaotic and changing society. His community is composed of opposing opinions, cultures, and traditions: Jews and Greeks, Christians and the newly converted, male, female, slave, and free. John tells them that "in the beginning was the Word, and the Word was with God, and the Word was God." For John, the gospel (good news) does not begin with angels proclaiming the birth of Jesus, but it begins with the Word. And if we are going to be effective with greeting others with hospitality, it should begin with the Word. The Apostle John knew this, as he was confronted with a divided community of Jews and Gentiles, both believing in Jesus; yet, still struggling to become unified as the body of Christ. For John, the solution was to find common ground between the two cultures through the Word. For the traditional Jews, the word *davar* represents the event by which the heavens and earth were created. For Greeks, the word *logos* meant "wisdom," which was more valued so than wealth. So, for John and his people, they could all agree that regardless of where each of us may come from, who each of us may have been, how long we may have been there, and doing whatever, when it comes to Jesus, He is the living Word of God. With that, we can then worship in the Word together, speak to God with the Word together, and speak to each with the Word together. And although the church is not the Word, we should be a voice. The Word of God is cradled in Christ's church. As attendants to that cradle, we have, at times, been abusive nannies. We have neglected the Word for ideologies and philosophies. We have abused the Word, often using it to keep others out, down, or in line. Some have even abandoned the Word for tradition or for prosperity. The church, the community of believers, is called to be a voice, the "shofar," the griot, the compass, and GPS for others to find their

Appendix H

way. That can only happen by getting our tongues under control and beginning to speak the Word of Life. Everything we do as the people of God should be concerning the Word of Life.

So how do we speak words of life? Since "death and life are in the power of the tongue," then how can we bring life to a church of empty pews, frustrated pastors, and complacent members with a complicit attitude? How do we truly begin to greet each other and strangers with the peace of the Lord?

The writer of 1 John says that they declare what was from the beginning, what they have heard, seen with their eyes, what they have looked at and touched their hands concerning the word of life. Well, what was it that they heard, saw, and touched? They saw and witnessed how God so loved the world through his Son, Jesus. They saw how that *Love* touched and healed lepers, blind people, and a woman with an issue of blood. They witnessed how *Love* fed thousands with a few loaves of bread and fish. They witnessed how, although he was mocked, beaten, and crucified, *Love* was still able to forgive. They witnessed *Love*. And, if we are to speak words of life so that others may have fellowship with us, we must begin with words of *Love*. First Corinthians 13:1: "If I speak in the tongues of men and of angels but have not love, I am only a resounding gong or a clanging cymbal. If I have the gift of prophecy and can fathom all mysteries and all knowledge, and if I have a faith that can move mountains but have not love, I am nothing. If I give all I possess to the poor and surrender my body to the flames, but have not love, I gain nothing." Martin Luther King once said that "love is the only force capable of transforming an enemy into a friend." And when it comes to speaking words of hospitality, we must transform each other with love.

Then we should speak with *integrity*: Say what you mean and mean what you say. God told the prophet, Isaiah, in 29:13, that "these people come near to me with their mouths and honor me with their lips, but their hearts are far from me" because they lack integrity. Their actions negated their words. They had no follow-through. That's why the writer in proverbs says, "The integrity of the upright guides them, but the unfaithful are destroyed by their duplicity." We must be a people who not only talk the talk but walk the walk, as well. Jesus kept and still keeps his word. Lord, help us to be a people who can keep our word.

Then we must learn to speak in faith: for church folks, this is one of the ultimate challenges. It astonishes me how people of the faith often speak

Sermon

words of fear and incapability. "Pastor, I'm afraid that we may not be able to take that on at this time." "Pastor, we need to be careful about whom we let join our church. They need to be for us." "Pastor, we're counting on you to bring in the new members because we all are not trained to tell others about Jesus." We have a tendency to first speak out of fear and our incapability. But God did not give us the spirit of fear. And furthermore, if we just simply learn how to love more, we would understand there is no love in fear. No wonder the great dreamer, Martin Luther King, could say, "Like anybody, I would like to have a long life. Longevity has its place. But I'm not concerned about that now. I just want to do God's will." Because he lived a life of love.

Finally, I'm learning that we, as followers of Christ, do not know how to speak words that lift people up and encourage them. We do know how to tear them down. We don't know how to give honor where honor is due. So, we need to allow the spirit of the Lord to teach us how to be encouragers through speaking words of life. "But encourage one another daily, as long as it is called today, so that none of you may be hardened by sin's deceitfulness" (Heb 3:13).

I recall a young woman who went to work one morning, not knowing that her words would make a difference in someone else's life. You may remember that young woman named Antoinette Tuff.

(Show video clip about Antoinette Tuff.)

Antoinette spoke words of LIFE (love, integrity, faith, and encouragement) into someone who not only wanted to end the lives of others but his own. We never know who God brings into our midst, but when they come, let's speak the words of LIFE. Words have power; let us be the messengers of His love not only through our deeds but also our words and how we use them. We can make our congregation a true sanctuary for all.

Appendix I

Sermon

Hospitality through Equality and Equity

Scripture: Matthew 20:1-16

When I first moved to North Plainfield, New Jersey, one of the most amazing things I marveled at was how some Latino men looking for work would gather on the corners of downtown wearing their painters' outfits and carrying an assortment of handyman tools. They would simply wait for business contractors, plumbers, and other companies to stop, choose a few of them, and take them on random jobs. All day, these day laborers as young as teenagers, often undereducated, unskilled, and often undocumented, would stand and simply hope and wait that they would get chosen to work for a few hours and get paid some money. Now, many would claim that they were undercutting job opportunities for American workers, and some could have been illegal aliens; yet, these were people willing to do an honest day's work. They had a thirst for that American dream of financial opportunity. And it is that thirst for access to the American dream that is in danger of being eliminated through our country's strife over immigration laws and border walls.

These day laborers seek to be included in that promise of happiness and prosperity that the founders of this country declared. And as our government is currently at a stalemate over inclusion for DACA, migrant workers, and those seeking asylum, it seems that the struggle for inclusion and equity has always been an issue within our society. It's only been less than one hundred fifty years since African Americans received the constitutional rights of equality, fifty years for women, and less than five years for marriage equality. Even though we live in a nation where all people are supposed to be created equal, for some of us, we are uncertain as to what that equality should look like. Moreover, in the kingdom of heaven, we seem not to grasp the concept that in Christ there is neither Jew nor Gentile, neither slave nor free, nor is there male and female, for we are all one in Christ Jesus.

It seems that in the church, we often get a little puffed up and elevated by thinking that there are some sinners who are less than others. You know, our sin isn't as bad and evil as their sin. When considering the consequences of our poor decisions, we often feel a little better knowing that we are not as bad as some other folks. I may be a liar, but thank God I'm not lazy. I may be a thief, but at least I'm not a drunk. I may be a womanizer, but at least I'm not gay. I may have different men fathering my children, but at least I'm not a prostitute. It seems that we are always comparing our lack of sin to the abundance of sin in others. After all, we are different from those folks. We go to church. We pay our tithes. We serve on various committees and boards. So, in our hearts, we echo the statement of the pharisee to the tax collector, "God, I thank you that I am not like other people: thieves, rogues, adulterers, or even like this tax collector." We commit the sin of judgment and cast bitterness and hate on others. But I'm reminded of the following words from Martin Luther King's "I Have A Dream Speech," where he said, "In the process of gaining our rightful place we must not be guilty of wrongful deeds. Let us not seek to satisfy our thirst for freedom by drinking from the cup of bitterness and hatred."[1]

And yet, as people of color striving for acceptability and respectability in White America, we tend to disapprove of those who do not fit into a paradigm of the White European heteronormative patriarchy. In fact, the more we succeed in becoming the model minority, the more we tend to oppress and depress those who do not. Just as we've been looked down upon, kept back from opportunities, and passed over because of our race and/or gender, we have a tendency to do the same to others, especially in the church. Liberationist Paulo Freire once stated that "the oppressed instead of striving for liberation tend themselves to become oppressors."[2] Malcolm X echoed those words of caution, saying that "if we are not careful, the

---

1. King, "I Have a Dream," para 8.
2. Freire, *Pedagogy of the Oppressed*, 45.

Appendix I

newspapers will have us hating the people who are being oppressed and loving the people who are doing the oppressing."[3] And it seems to be just the case. Many of us have allowed some of the mass media to stir up in us a disdain for oppressed people, and we too participate in the oppression. We turn our noses up to those who do not measure up to the American image of acceptability; for instance, the group of boys with the pants around their knees, the young baby mommas with multiple children, the homeless vets and gay youth living on the streets, and people struggling with addiction. These are the unwanted, the unacceptable, the overlooked, the outcast, and not the model sheep that churches often seek and want to add to their fold. We who have been oppressed have become the oppressors of others. We have allowed the world standards of respectability and acceptability to replace the gospel of reconciliation and restoration and God is not pleased.

The Gospel of Matthew gives us a divine lesson on equality and equity. Although our God is one of impartiality, the Lord is also one of grace. And there are some of us that tend to need a little more grace than others. That is why the scriptures state that his love covers a multitude of sins because, for some of us, who would have drowned in the depths of our iniquity, there may be a need for more grace than for others. It's not that we are favored or preferred, but it's because God desires to see no one person perish. And often, to raise us up above the waters of our transgressions, God may have to dive in just a little deeper to get us. Justice would have required equal treatment, but unmerited grace dictates mercy and compassion. In God's kingdom, the scales of Justice are balanced with grace and mercy.

The writer of Matthew knew this as he himself required that grace and mercy in his life. As he retells these parables and incidents of Jesus, we are also seeing his spiritual journey with Jesus through every line. As a tax collector, he knew what it meant to be despised and rejected by others. Now I must confess that out of all the New Testament writers, I have a penchant for Matthew. I identify with his former profession of tax collecting or managing the account receivables for a government body. As a business manager for the large institution of Princeton University, I can understand some of the challenges that Matthew must have dealt with when confronting people who owed money. Now, if you want to see some of the worse sides of humanity, try to separate people from their money. Matthew had to deal with the rough personalities of people as he took their money and placed it into the coffers of the government. That's a difficult job to do while going

---

3. Malcolm X, quoted in Epps, "Rhetoric of Malcom X," 70.

around town and shaking down widows, poor farmers, and the under-caste for what was owed to Cesar. He was like the modern-day repo-man who is despised and rejected as he tries to make a living. So, I have a special place in my heart for Matthew because I've been there and done that in my career as I too had to collect money from students, parents (trying to pay for college), or drug addicts, ex-cons, and prostitutes (trying to pay for rehab) and even now while working at Princeton, I collected from nonprofit and religious organizations who owe money for services rendered. And the one thing they all have in common is they transfer their anger and frustrations onto the person taking their money. So, I can imagine how Matthew must have felt being humiliated, being hated by your countrymen because you were working for the enemy, and not quite fitting in with the enemy (Rome) because you were a Jew. It's no wonder when Jesus of Nazareth comes along to his table neither judging nor condemning him, but saying, "Come join me"—Matthew jumps up without question and follows Christ. Jesus invites Matthew to be a part of his world, his team, his family of fishermen, rebels, and thieves. I believe that Matthew understands what it really means to be hated, marginalized, and ostracized by people yet chosen, loved, and affirmed by Jesus. He knows what it means to be left out of society, yet called to be included in the kingdom. So, when he recounts this parable of Jesus comparing the kingdom of heaven to that of a landowner going out every two to three hours within a day into the marketplace to get workers for his vineyard, we get a glimpse of God's equity as compared to our sense of equality.

Listen to the complaints of the workers who worked all day yet received the same amount of compensation as those who just worked an hour. "These last worked only one hour, and you have made them equal to us who have borne the burden of the day and the scorching heat." For the workers who have been there all day, there appears to be an injustice. They see the injustice of values. For them, they feel that they should be rewarded for their longevity in the vineyard. They see the injustice of rules. They agreed to the terms for compensation yet are displeased when others are awarded the same. They see the injustice of implementation. They were hired first yet got paid last. They see the injustice of decision-making. The accusation to the landowner is that "you have made them equal to us." And that is the crux of the problem for every church seeking to grow. The mentality that seniority, longevity, rank, and title translate into greater reward and recognition in the kingdom is errant.

Appendix I

Jesus tells us that in the kingdom of heaven, seniority does not give way to priority. Just because you've been serving the longest does mean that you get priority or preferred treatment in God's kingdom. Remember that Jesus told the disciples that even John the Baptist would be least in the kingdom. And although we sit and nod our heads in agreement, when it comes to the reality of our churches in general, there are those who would consciously argue for the defense of "seasoned members" over "newcomers" or even "outsiders." That's why we will argue, "Well, you know, Brother Johnson has been a contributing member of this church for years, and we hold him in high regard, so you have to give way. We don't know anything about these other people coming into our church. Some of them are not even members. And besides, we need to take care of family first." Or, this ministry was here before that ministry. We should have priority over that ministry since we have done more for the church. And as a result, God's church takes on a "cliquish" attitude. It is an "us against them" attitude. And the reason we think like that is that we have allowed the world's standards to either supersede or replace God's standards and practices for his kingdom. We have brought the world's philosophy of the lack of justice, equality, and fair play into God's church.

Jesus goes on to show us the sovereignty of God. That's why the saints sang, "Salvation belongs to our God who is seated on the throne, and to the Lamb!" Salvation is his and his alone. Look at who Jesus incorporated into his ministry: fishermen—who cussed and fought all the time, an unpopular tax collector, a lying thief, women who once were demon-filled, and prostitutes. Jesus employs whoever, whenever, wherever, however, and for whatever because he is the head of the church. He writes the job descriptions and signs the paychecks for his kingdom. Why? Because God's thoughts are not our thoughts and God's ways are not our ways, we must be open to the possibility of grace by accepting a different set of values and standards for procedures in the kingdom. As long as we insist on the equality of the exchange, we will not be able to accept grace. God's grace gives equity where there are challenges preventing us from achieving goals on unlevel grounds. Here is what we need to understand. Equality suggests that everyone is at an exact starting point and should be treated the same. It seeks to promote fairness, but it can only work if everyone starts from the same place and needs the same level of support.

Equity, by way of contrast, aims to give everyone what they need to be successful. It focuses on equality of outcomes. This involves considering structures that might put certain groups at a disadvantage. Equality aims to promote fairness, but it can only work if everyone starts from the same place and needs the same aid. Equity, on the face of it, *appears* unfair, but it actively moves everyone closer to success by "leveling the playing field." It is important to recognize that not everyone starts at the same place, and not everyone has the same needs. And yet, to give us access to the Tree of Life, God's grace stands in the gap to make up the difference.

And, unless we elevate our attitudes from the belief of entitlement because we are the "elect of God" predestined for heaven, we will never be able to engage others effectively. And quoting scriptures to justify keeping others out of the church and offices is an abuse of power. It has already been done. It was done with the Catholic Church to justify conquering the Americas and Africa to tame the unsaved savages. It was done by American Protestants to keep slavery enforced with "slaves be obedient to your masters." It was done by the church to keep women out of leadership. Now, it continues to be done to keep LGBTQ people out of the church and leadership. And now that our society has been empowered to google scriptures for themselves, your interpretation of the Bible to keep others out is no longer viable. We must elevate our minds from the thoughts of entitlement so that we can effectively engage everyone.

The disgruntled workers accuse the landowner of "equality," saying, "You have made them equal to us . . ." Something shifted whereby those who were once the unwanted yet willing are now equal to those who had the privilege of being first. We know this when initially approached by the landowner, the last hired, the unwanted responded: "No one will hire us." What was it about them that no one wanted?

- Were they too old? That's ageism.
- Were they not the right gender? That's sexism.
- Were they not the right skin color? That's racism.
- Were they not the right culture or citizenship? That's xenophobia.
- Were they not the right sexual orientation? That's homophobia.
- Were there some physical limitations to their abilities? That's ableism.

We are not sure what the circumstances were behind the fact that no one hired this group, but we do know that the landowner thought that this last group was worthy of inclusion.

Appendix I

    This preacher believes that the determining factor was their attitude. I believe that the landowner was willing to pay these eleventh-hour workers the same wage because of their attitude of faith. Think about it. These day laborers stood in the marketplace until 5 p.m. toward the end of the workday. For some reason or another, these workers still had some optimism that someone would come along and hire them. They never lost hope. Oh, you don't hear me. The landowner, God, was willing to add them to the Lord's labor force because they had faith. The long wait in the marketplace did not make them bitter or rude. The delay in God's showing up did not cause them to doubt or show disappointment. They didn't grumble or gripe. And that's a quality we need for all our laborers in God's vineyard. If we had more workers who did less grumbling and showed more gratitude, the church would be bursting at the seams. We need workers who will never lose hope, who know what it means to believe that "they that wait on the Lord, shall renew their strength; they shall mount up with wings as eagles; they shall run, and not be weary, and they shall walk, and not faint."

    Regardless of what the circumstances may look like, regardless of how little you may have, regardless of how many times people may tell you no, never lose hope. Oh, you don't hear me. I don't know about you, but at 5:00 p.m. at Princeton, we are shutting down computers, turning off lights, and packing up for home. Yet, these day laborers were still hoping for a hire. These workers were rewarded because of their belief that something would occur. That's the attitude we all need as we continue to work for the kingdom. The good news is that God may not come when you want him, but he will show up on time. Sometimes that maybe even within the last hour. Keep an attitude of hope and faith. Let our attitude be one of continual hope.

Appendix J

RICH One-on-One Interviews

With the exception of the interview with the pastor of TBC, the following interviews were labeled and written to protect the identities of the interviewees. Therefore, the names RICH-1, RICH-2, RICH-3, and RICH-4 were used.

RICH-1 Interview

RICH-1: The message was powerful and timely because we had a church meeting yesterday. It was what could have been the onset of World War III at TBC. Everything you preach that TBC should strive for—love, integrity, faith, and encouragement—was lacking. I left that meeting discouraged and wondered how much more I could take. There was a lot of disrespectful words said to the pastor by church members, and I was embarrassed for him. So, I felt your message was so timely and definitely straight from the throne of God.

Researcher: Thank you for that. You have attended several of the workshops and heard many of the sermons on hospitality. How would you describe the tone of TBC with dealing with the newcomers?

RICH-1: It has gotten better. Prior to Pastor Bembry's arrival, there was a time when there was a group of people who ran the church and dictated what went on in TBC. They were very

Appendix J

	exclusive, and you had to seek permission to get certain ministries and activities going for the youth and other concerns. So, where we were then and where we are now is totally different under Pastor Bembry's leadership. Now I think we are very receptive to bringing new people into TBC. People are paying attention to what is happening around TBC. With the various messages being preached about globalization, gentrification, and inclusion, I think that their eyes are being opened. There still may be some people who are reluctant. But, overall, I think the majority of TBC is receptive.
Researcher:	What would you say is the attitude regarding the LGBTQ community?
RICH-1:	I think that there are some at TBC who are very receptive to all people, but there are some who are not as receptive. I can't say that it is homophobia, but I do know that they are not at that place where many of us are when it comes to being inclusive. We are all people regardless of who you are. I didn't choose to be Black. So why would anyone try to exclude me from this space?
Researcher:	So, what would occur if a same-sex male couple came into TBC with two children?
RICH-1:	I think people would be hospitable. I really believe that. We have had members who were a part of the LGBTQ community, male and female, in the choir and different parts of the church. And this was prior to marriage equality. People understood what that meant. People were afraid to speak of who they were. But they were very much embraced.
Researcher:	What about those same persons getting involved in decision-making committees and positions?
RICH-1:	I think that there may be some who would object, but I think the masses would still be receptive. Very recently we had a praise and worship leader who relocated to New Jersey with a new job. But he was loved and embraced by all.

RICH One-on-One Interviews

Researcher: So, would you say that the atmosphere in TBC is one where they do not speak on the matter, like the elephant in the room?

RICH-1: No, they will speak on it. We once had a young man working on his internship for ministry, and then he got married. It was a same-sex marriage. And people spoke up about it. He never came back. He was here for a while; he was a part of our youth ministry. Having him here was fine until he got married. As I said, very few people became confrontational about it. It wasn't done in a loving kind of way.

Researcher: So, do you think with more preaching on LGBTQ issues and more advocacy more people would come around?

RICH-1: As a minister, I believe so. In the messages that I preach and teach, I always try to be inclusive. I believe that I do advocate. I believe that as a preacher we all need advocates. I think it is important.

RICH-2 Interview

RICH-2: I've noticed in this church that if you are not of a particular class or can't contribute toward a committee, people tend to ignore you.

Researcher: How does that make you feel?

RICH-2: It makes you feel like you're nothing, and often you don't feel like you want to be in church.

Researcher: So how long have you been a member of this church?

RICH-2: Since the 1990s but I didn't take fellowship until this pastor came.

Researcher: You shared with me previously that you have a family member in the LGBTQ community. Have you shared this with anyone in TBC?

Appendix J

RICH-2: I've shared it with only one person, and that is my deaconess. No one else in this church knows about this—not even the pastor.

Researcher: How does it make you feel not being able to share this information? Do you feel ashamed?

RICH-2: No, I'm not ashamed of my grandchild. It is just that people at TBC like to gossip. My daughter is ashamed. She is so Pentecostal. When I told her about you, she said to me, they should not allow him to preach because it is like they are saying it is alright. I said I make my own decisions. When my grandchild came out and told his parents about his sexuality, he had to move out. He was living on the streets and in some home for gay youth for a while until I convinced him to move in with me. I always knew that he was gay. His parents were in denial. When they were talking about moving to Jamaica, I told my grandson that it would not be safe for him. Even here in Brooklyn, he was attacked on the streets one day. But his mother would just nag and nag him until he left, and I convinced him to move in with me. [The interviewee went on to describe in her own words about her grandson transitioning into a woman. She indicated that she observed him wearing wigs, nails, and women's clothing.] He has even changed his name.

Researcher: So, it seems that it is not the homosexuality that is only the problem; it is the transsexuality of your grandchild that your daughter is dealing with?

RICH-2: Yes, he is taking hormones now and has taken a girl's name. That is the problem. So, they don't want to see him. But this past Thanksgiving I invited him to dinner. So, I'm trying to get them together. But the other issue is that my other son is a pastor and told her to fast and pray about it.

[The interviewee became slightly emotional. At this point, the researcher shared his own story about how some of his family members excluded him, as well.]

RICH One-on-One Interviews

Researcher:	As a word of encouragement, I will say that it is important that as your grandchild transitions, it is essential that someone in his family begins to acknowledge the new identity as far as the new name and pronouns. Have you had that conversation yet?
RICH-2:	That is why I'm engaging, and honestly, I'm struggling with the new name. But my issue is that I want my grandchild to go to college. My child is working, but I want him to have a degree. He says that he will go, but I don't see it happening.
Researcher:	Could it be that your grandchild is waiting for the completion of his transition? After all, it would be easier to enter that environment after the process is done.
RICH-2:	It could be. I didn't think of it like that.
Researcher:	So here is the final question. Do you think that TBC would become a place that you would feel comfortable to invite your grandchild?
RICH-2:	I don't think so. Not with these people.

The researcher ended the interview with prayer.

RICH-3 Interview

RICH-3:	When we joined here, the pastor just got here, and the congregation was aging. But I have noticed that this church has grown spiritually in worship. They used just to be conservative and quiet. But they have grown to become more expressive in the worship service.
Researcher:	During the RICH we talked about being authentic in conversations with others. Do you think TBC can surpass its stereotype about being a homophobic church against the LGBTQ community?
RICH-3:	I think that TBC has opened its doors more toward other people. When my husband and I first came to TBC, it was

Appendix J

a cold church, but I did not feel unwelcomed. After the service, many people did not associate with each other. But we felt that TBC was just the right size church for us. The pastor always preached about the necessity to get to know each other.

Researcher: As newcomers begin to come into TBC, how do you think they will be received?

RICH-3: TBC needs trained greeters that are versed in inclusivity so that people can be welcomed. I know that your workshops and sermons have caused me to think about people differently and how I use my words toward others. I think others within this church can benefit from that as well.

RICH-4 Interview

RICH-4: Your messages definitely have caused me to reflect on my marriage. I know that my spouse is aware of my sexuality. However, as long as I'm loving them and respecting them, my spouse is very accepting. I also believe my family knows but no one has said anything. But your messages have made me question my authenticity. Am I lying to people?

Researcher: Each person in the LGBTQ community has his and her own journey to self-discovery, so I can't answer that. But I can say for myself that I needed to be authentic in order to be the best instrument of God that I could be.

RICH-4: You are right. It is my journey.

RICH One-on-One Interviews

Pastor of TBC-Interview

Pastor: I need to affirm that your presence has unleashed some positive energy at TBC. The people are very enthusiastic. They are quoting you. They respect you and your intelligence. After eighteen years of pastoring, I have seen a change in TBC. I have to say that TBC has surprised me by accepting you as an openly gay minister. You have been teaching us about radical inclusion, and it seems that the Black Church should have been doing this for years.

Researcher: So, do you think that going through the various workshops and hearing the sermons, the participants were transformed?

Pastor: Oh, absolutely! We had a leadership meeting this past week, and of course, we were discussing you and giving you the right hand of fellowship, and so many of them began to talk about LGBTQ persons within their own families. And I've been the pastor here for eighteen years and learned that they have been withholding information like that from me. So, I'm learning that there is a perception within my leadership that had precluded them from disclosing that information.

Researcher: So, how do you get TBC to get comfortable with discussing those issues and having authentic conversations?

Pastor: My leaders said to me that they feel that they need to open up a dialogue about inclusiveness and the LGBTQ community. So, as far as where we go from here, we need to open the doors to a conversation about the issue.

Bibliography

Angelou, Maya. "Dr. Maya Angelou on the Power of Words | Oprah's Master Class | Oprah Winfrey Network." Recorded on OWN, May 28, 2014. YouTube video, 1:07. https://youtu.be/BKv65MdlV-c.
Askew, Emily, et al. *Beyond Heterosexism in the Pulpit*. Eugene, OR: Cascade, 2015. Kindle edition.
Anti-Violence Project. "AVP Learns of an Anti-Gay Incident in Downtown Brooklyn." *NYC Anti-Violence Project*. Last modified April 20, 2017. https://avp.org/avp-learns-anti-gay-incident-downtown-brooklyn/.
Badgett, M. V. Lee, and Jody L. Herman. *Patterns of Relationship Recognition by Same-Sex Couples in the United States*. November 2011. https://williamsinstitute.law.ucla.edu/wp-content/uploads/Relationship-Recog-SS-Couples-US-Nov-2011.pdf.
Bailey, Randall C., et al. *They Were Together in One Place? Toward Minority Biblical Criticism*. Atlanta: Society of Biblical Literature, 2009. Google Play Books edition.
Barksdale, Aaron. "Bishop T. D. Jakes on the Black Church's Shifting Stance on the LGBT Community." *Huffington Post*, December 20, 2016. https://www.huffingtonpost.com/entry/td-jakes-says-the-black-church-and-lgbt-community-can-absolutely-coexist_us_55c0cc80e4b0b23e3ce3ff7a.
Barnes, Sandra L. *Live Long and Prosper: How Black Megachurches Address HIV/AIDS and Poverty in the Age of Prosperity Theology*. New York: Fordham University Press, 2013. Google Play Books edition.
———. "To Welcome or Affirm: Black Clergy Views about Homosexuality, Inclusivity, and Church Leadership." *Journal of Homosexuality* 60 (September 2013) 1409–33.
Brathwaite, Les Fabian. "Less than 50% of Teens Identify as Straight, Says New Study." *OUT*, May 11, 2018. https://www.out.com/news-opinion/2016/3/11/less-50-teens-identify-straight-says-new-study.
Brown, Sally A, and Luke A Powery. *Ways of the Word: Learning to Preach for Your Time and Place*. Minneapolis: Fortress, 2016.
Capretto, Lisa. "Dr. Maya Angelou on the Power of Words (Video)." *Huffington Post*, June 6, 2014. http://www.huffingtonpost.com/2014/06/06/maya-angelou-power-of-words_n_5462077.html.
Chadee, Derek, et al. "Religiosity and Attitudes towards Homosexuals in a Caribbean Environment." *Social and Economic Studies* 62 (June 2013) 1–28. www.jstor.org/stable/24384494.
Chapell, Bryan. *Christ-Centered Preaching: Redeeming the Expository Sermon*. Grand Rapids: Baker Academic, 2005. Kindle edition.

Bibliography

Cheng, Patrick S. *From Sin to Amazing Grace: Discovering the Queer Christ.* New York: Seabury, 2012. Google Play Books edition.

———. *Radical Love: An Introduction to Queer Theology.* New York: Seabury, 2011. Google Play Books edition.

The Church of Jesus Christ of Latter-day Saints (CJCLDS). "A Good Samaritan." YouTube video, 5:44. November 16, 2017. https://youtu.be/knujQ81iWjk.

———. "Peter's Revelation to Take the Gospel to the Gentiles." YouTube video, 9:06. July 25, 2013. https://www.youtube.com/watch?v=HeEUuzU9MQg.

Comstock, Garry D., and Susan E. Henking. *Que(e)Rying Religion: A Critical Anthology.* New York: Continuum, 1999.

Cone, James H. *Black Theology and Black Power.* Maryknoll: Orbis, 1997.

———. *A Black Theology of Liberation.* Maryknoll: Orbis, 2017.

———. *Speaking the Truth: Ecumenism, Liberation, and Black Theology.* Grand Rapids: Eerdmans, 1986.

———. "Theology's Great Sin: Silence in the Face of White Supremacy." *Black Theology* 2 (2004) 139–52. https://www.tandfonline.com/doi/abs/10.1558/blth.2.2.139.36027.

Cone, James H., and Gayraud S. Wilmore. *Black Theology: A Documentary History.* Vol. 2. Maryknoll: Orbis, 1993.

Constantine-Simms, Delroy, and Horace Griffin. "Their Own Received Them Not." In *The Greatest Taboo: Homosexuality in Black Communities,* 110–21. Los Angeles: Alyson, 2001.

Corasaniti, Nick, et al. "Church Massacre Suspect Held as Charleston Grieves." *New York Times,* June 18, 2015. https://www.nytimes.com/2015/06/19/us/charleston-church-shooting.html.

Crenshaw, Kimberlé. "Why Intersectionality Can't Wait." *Washington Post,* September 24, 2015. https://www.washingtonpost.com/news/in-theory/wp/2015/09/24/why-intersectionality-cant-wait/?utm_term=.54e21fcc560b.

Dyson, Michael Eric. *Tears We Cannot Stop: A Sermon to White America.* New York: St. Martin's, 2017. Kindle edition.

Enrico. "Parable of the Vineyard Workers." *Vimeo.* Uploaded May 10, 2017. https://vimeo.com/216811415.

Epps, Archie C. "The Rhetoric of Malcolm X." *Harvard Review* 3 (1993) 64–75. http://www.jstor.org/stable/27559632.

Freire, Paulo. *Pedagogy of the Oppressed.* New York: Continuum, 2005.

Gast, Phil. "Obama Announces He Supports Same-Sex Marriage." *CNN,* May 9, 2012. https://www.cnn.com/2012/05/09/politics/obama-same-sex-marriage/index.html.

Gates, Gary J. "How Many People Are Lesbian, Gay, Bisexual and Transgender?" *Williams Institute.* March 28, 2013. https://williamsinstitute.law.ucla.edu/publications/how-many-people-lgbt/.

"Gay Realtor Brooklyn, New York—Top Gay Neighborhoods." *Gay Real Estate.* https://www.gayrealestate.com/news/usa/new-york/brooklyn/gay-realtor-brooklyn-new-york-top-gay-neighborhoods.html.

Gewurz, Danielle. "Growing Support for Gay Marriage: Changed Minds and Changing Demographics." *Pew Research Center.* March 20, 2013. http://www.people-press.org/2013/03/20/growing-support-for-gay-marriage-changed-minds-and-changing-demographics/.

Bibliography

Glaude, Eddie. "The Black Church Is Dead." *Huffington Post*, April 26, 2010. http://www.huffingtonpost.com/eddie-glaude-jr-phd/the-black-church-is-dead_b_473815.html.

Glaude, Eddie, et al. "Is the Black Church Dead? A Roundtable on the Future of Black Churches." Roundtable conversation, Columbia University, January 13, 2012. YouTube video, 2:02:05. https://www.youtube.com/watch?v=7r8Djfxu1Bk.

Gonzalez, Justo L., and Catherine Gonzalez. *The Liberating Pulpit*. Nashville: Abingdon, 1994. Google Play Books edition.

Goodman, Matt, ed. "Accelerating Acceptance 2018." *GLAAD*. January 25, 2018. https://www.glaad.org/publications/accelerating-acceptance-2018.

Goss, Robert E., and Mona West. *Take Back the Word: A Queer Reading of the Bible*. Cleveland: Pilgrim, 2001.

Gould, Meredith. *The Social Media Gospel: Sharing the Good News in New Ways*. Collegeville: Liturgical, 2015. Kindle edition.

Graybill, Rhiannon. "Thematic Guide: LGBTQ Sexuality and the Hebrew Bible." *Oxford Biblical Studies Online*. April 2015. http://www.oxfordbiblicalstudies.com/resource/lgbtq_bible.xhtml.

Griffin, Horace L. *Their Own Receive Them Not: African American Lesbians and Gays in Black Churches*. Eugene, OR: Wipf & Stock, 2010.

Hahn, Heather. "Church Lacks Racial Diversity Officials Say." *United Methodist News Service*. September 20, 2010. https://www.umnews.org/en/news/church-lacks-racial-diversity-officials-say.

———. "Ethnic Diversity Critical to Church Future." *United Methodist News Service*. December 4, 2012. https://www.umnews.org/en/news/ethnic-diversity-critical-to-church-future.

Hanway, Donald G. *A Theology of Gay and Lesbian Inclusion: Love Letters to the Church*. Binghamton, NY: Haworth Pastoral, 2006.

Hawkins, Lynette. "Church Hospitality Training with Lynette Hawkins." YouTube video, 1:52. July 24, 2011. https://youtu.be/rJlIsT1SnHs.

Helsel, Carolyn Browning. "Queering 'Straight' Preaching." *Theology & Sexuality* 19 (April 2015) 11–20.

Hobbs, Steven H. "Following the Drum Major for Justice: Reflections on Luther D. Ivory's *Toward a Theology of Radical Involvement: The Theological Legacy of Martin Luther King, Jr.*" *Alabama Law Review* 50 (1998) 7–37. https://www.law.ua.edu/lawreview/archives/volume-50/.

Howard, Jacqueline. "Americans Devote More Than 10 Hours a Day to Screen Time, and Growing." *CNN*, July 29, 2016. https://www.cnn.com/2016/06/30/health/americans-screen-time-nielsen/index.html.

Jayson, Sharon. "Gender Loses Its Impact with the Young." *USA Today*, June 21, 2014. https://www.usatoday.com/story/news/nation/2014/06/21/gender-millennials-dormitories-sex/10573099/.

Jefferson, Thomas. "The Declaration of Independence: Full Text." 1776. Available online at http://www.ushistory.org/Declaration/document/.

Jensen, Richard A. *Envisioning the Word: The Use of Visual Images in Preaching*. Minneapolis: Fortress, 2005.

Johnson, E. Patrick. "Feeling the Spirit in the Dark." In *The Greatest Taboo: Homosexuality in Black Communities*, edited by Delroy Constantine-Simms, 88–109. Los Angeles: Alyson, 2000.

Bibliography

Johnson, Jay. "Biblical Sexuality and Gender: Renewing Christian Witness to the Gospel." *CLGS*. August 11, 2011. https://clgs.org/multimedia-archive/biblical-sexuality-and-gender-renewing-christian-witness-to-the-gospel/.

Joyce, Rosemary. "Fear of the Other: An Anti-American Position." *Berkeley Blog*. August 23, 2010. https://blogs.berkeley.edu/2010/08/23/fear-of-the-other-an-anti-american-position/.

King, Coretta Scott. "1996 Atlanta Gay Pride Festival Speech by Coretta Scott King." YouTube video, 9:55. October 7, 2009. https://www.youtube.com/watch?v=bHm8djZqTzk.

King, J. L. *On the Down Low: A Journey into the Lives of "Straight" Black Men Who Sleep with Men*. New York: Broadway, 2004.

King, Martin Luther. *A Gift of Love: Sermons from* Strength to Love *and Other Preachings*. Boston: Beacon, 2012. Kindle edition.

———. "'I Have a Dream,' Address Delivered at the March on Washington for Jobs and Freedom." Address delivered August 28, 1963. Available online at https://kinginstitute.stanford.edu/king-papers/documents/i-have-dream-address-delivered-march-washington-jobs-and-freedom.

———. "The Most Segregated Hour in America—Martin Luther King Jr." Meet the Press, April 17, 1960. YouTube video, 0:52. https://youtu.be/1q881g1L_d8.

———. *A Testament of Hope: The Essential Writings and Speeches of Martin Luther King, Jr.* Edited by James Melvin Washington. San Francisco: HarperOne, 1991.

Koeshall, Dan. "Nothing Can Separate Us from the Love of God." *LGBTWeekly.com*, January 17, 2013. http://lgbtweekly.com/2013/01/17/nothing-can-separate-us-from-the-love-of-god/. Article no longer available.

Kuile, Casper ter. "Millennials Haven't Forgotten Spirituality, They're Just Looking for New Venues." PBS News Hour, March 3, 2017. YouTube video, 3:14. https://youtu.be/lqE9TqUzrtc.

Leonhardt, David. "New York Still Has More Gay Residents Than Anywhere Else in the U.S." *New York Times*, March 23, 2015. https://www.nytimes.com/2015/03/24/upshot/new-york-still-has-more-gay-residents-than-anywhere-else-in-us.html.

LeTourneau, Nancy. "'Until Justice Rolls Down Like Waters.'" *Washington Monthly*, November 28, 2014. https://washingtonmonthly.com/2014/11/28/until-justice-rolls-down-like-waters-2/.

Lipka, Michael. "Many U.S. Congregations Are Still Racially Segregated, but Things Are Changing." *Pew Research Center*. December 8, 2014. http://www.pewresearch.org/fact-tank/2014/12/08/many-u-s-congregations-are-still-racially-segregated-but-things-are-changing-2/.

———. "The Most and Least Racially Diverse U.S. Religious Groups." *Pew Research Center*, July 27, 2015. https://www.pewresearch.org/fact-tank/2015/07/27/the-most-and-least-racially-diverse-u-s-religious-groups/.

Logue, Frank. "The 6 Minutes That Matter Most to Church Visitors." YouTube video, 0:55. Posted April 9, 2017. https://youtu.be/J-0orTBE5sU.

Loue, Sana. *Understanding Theology and Homosexuality in African American Communities*. New York: Springer, 2014.

Maxwell, John C. *The 21 Most Powerful Minutes in a Leader's Day*. Nashville: Nelson, 2000.

McLeod, Kimberley. "Taking a Lead on Faith: Four Black Pastors at the Forefront of LGBT Equality." *Ebony*, January 30, 2012. https://www.ebony.com/faith_spirituality/taking-a-lead-on-faith-four-black-pastors-at-the-forefront-of-lgbt-equality/.

Bibliography

McNeill, John J. *Taking a Chance on God: Liberating Theology for Gays, Lesbians, and Their Lovers, Families, and Friends; With a New Preface.* Boston: Beacon, 1996.

Miller, Robert L. "Legacy Denied: African American Gay Men, AIDS, and the Black Church." *Social Work* 52 (January 2007) 51–61. https://academic.oup.com/sw/article-abstract/52/1/51/1943652?redirectedFrom=fulltext.

Mink, Michael D., et al. "Stress, Stigma, and Sexual Minority Status: The Intersectional Ecology Model of LGBTQ Health." *Journal of Gay & Lesbian Social Services* 26 (November 2014) 502–21. https://www.tandfonline.com/doi/abs/10.1080/10538720.2014.953660.

Murphy, Caryle. "More U.S. Christians OK with Homosexuality." *Pew Research Center.* December 18, 2015. http://www.pewresearch.org/fact-tank/2015/12/18/most-u-s-christian-groups-grow-more-accepting-of-homosexuality/.

Newbell, Trillia. "Why Diversity in Church Is about More Than Race." Good Book Company, June 28, 2017. YouTube video, 1:17. https://youtu.be/-WPM8KmcoMY.

Nieman, James R., and Thomas G. Rogers. *Preaching to Every Pew: Cross Cultural Strategies.* Minneapolis: Fortress, 2001. Kindle edition.

Nouwen, Henri J. M. *Reaching Out.* New York: Doubleday, 1975. Google Play Books edition.

———. *The Wounded Healer: Ministry in Contemporary Society.* New York: Image, 1979.

Parker, Brianna K. "One Size Does Not Fit All: Black Millennials Demand More." *Christian Citizen.* August 2, 2017. https://medium.com/christian-citizen/one-size-does-not-fit-all-black-millennials-demand-more-b5555cfb9b7c.

Pearson, Carlton. *The Gospel of Inclusion: Reaching beyond Religious Fundamentalism to the True Love of God and Self.* New York: Atria, 2006. Google Play Books edition.

Pinn, Anthony B. *Terror and Triumph: The Nature of Black Religion.* Minneapolis: Fortress, 2003.

Prahlad, Anand. *The Greenwood Encyclopedia of African American Folklore.* Westport, CT: Greenwood, 2006.

Proctor, Samuel D. *The Certain Sound of the Trumpet: Crafting a Sermon of Authority.* Valley Forge, PA: Judson, 1994.

Quanbeck, Philip A., II. "PowerPoint in Preaching? No!" *Word & World* 28 (Fall 2008) 420, 422. https://wordandworld.luthersem.edu/content/pdfs/28-4_A_Cloud_of_Witnesses/28-4_Face_to_Face.pdf.

Rainer, Thom S., and Jess W. Rainer. *The Millennials: Connecting to America's Largest Generation.* Nashville: B&H, 2011.

Reaves, Jayme R. *Safeguarding the Stranger: An Abrahamic Theology and Ethic of Protective Hospitality.* Eugene, OR: Pickwick, 2016. Kindle edition.

Rodriguez, Eric M. "At the Intersection of Church and Gay: A Review of the Psychological Research on Gay and Lesbian Christians." *Journal of Homosexuality* 57 (January 2010) 5–38. https://www.periodicals.com/stock_e/j/ttl51747.html.

Rogers, Fred. "Mr. Rogers Won't You Be My Neighbor?" https://www.misterrogers.org/watch/.

Root, Andrew. "PowerPoint in Preaching? Yes . . . But!" *Word & World* 28 (Fall 2008) 421, 423. https://wordandworld.luthersem.edu/content/pdfs/28-4_A_Cloud_of_Witnesses/28-4_Face_to_Face.pdf.

Russell, Letty M. *Just Hospitality: God's Welcome in a World of Difference.* Louisville: Westminster John Knox, 2009. Google Play Books edition.

Russell, Thaddeus. "The Color of Discipline: Civil Rights and Black Sexuality." *American Quarterly* 60 (2008) 101–28. http://www.jstor.org/stable/40068501.

Bibliography

Samuels, Herbert, and Mireille Miller-Young. "Sex Stereotypes of African Americans Have Long History." *NPR*, May 7, 2007. https://www.npr.org/templates/story/story.php?storyId=10057104.

Sanders, Cody J. "Preaching Messages We Never Intended." *Theology & Sexuality* 19 (April 2015) 21–35.

Sanders, Cody J., and Angela Yarber. *Microaggressions in Ministry: Confronting the Hidden Violence of Everyday Church*. Louisville: Westminster John Knox, 2015. Kindle edition.

Sawyer, Garrett Michael. "Exploring Possibilities for LGBT Youth Programing in Religious Spaces: A Study of the Episcopal Church." MA thesis, University of Austin, May 2016. https://repositories.lib.utexas.edu/handle/2152/38166.

Skeldon, Grant. "Millennial Asks Pastor A. R. Bernard Why Millennials Are Leaving." YouTube video, 2:03. July 26, 2018. https://youtu.be/yokiGNjqyCo.

Slagter, Lauren. "LGBTQ Students at Christian Colleges Refuse to Choose between Sexuality and Faith." *MLive.com*. May 9, 2018. http://www.mlive.com/news/ann-arbor/index.ssf/page/refusing_to_choose_lgbtq_stude.html.

Sneed, Roger A. *Representations of Homosexuality*. New York: Palgrave Macmillan, 2010.

Spears-Newsome, Wesley. "6 Essentials for Churches Engaging Millennials." *Baptist News Global*. April 5, 2016. https://baptistnews.com/article/6-essentials-for-churches-engaging-millennials/#.WvY5Z4gvyM8.

Steele, Claude M. *Whistling Vivaldi: How Stereotypes Affect Us and What We Can Do*. New York: Norton, 2011.

Sutherland, Arthur. *I Was a Stranger: A Christian Theology of Hospitality*. Nashville: Abingdon, 2006. Google Play Books edition.

Travis, Sarah. "Troubled Gospel: Postcolonial Preaching for the Colonized, Colonizer, and Everyone in Between." *Homiletic Journal* 40 (2015) 46–54. https://ejournals.library.vanderbilt.edu/index.php/homiletic/article/view/4121.

Tuff, Antoinette. "Atlanta School Shooting: Antoinette Tuff Tells Alleged School Shooter She Loves Him in 911 Call." ABC News, August 22, 2013. YouTube video, 3:02. https://youtu.be/EfB70KKd68E?t=4.

Tutu, Desmond. "Our Glorious Diversity: Why We Should Celebrate Difference." *Huffington Post*, June 21, 2011. https://www.huffingtonpost.com/desmond-tutu/our-glorious-diversity-wh_b_874791.html.

US Census Bureau. "Crown Heights CDP, New York." https://data.census.gov/cedsci/profile?g=1600000US3619229.

———. "Millennials Outnumber Baby Boomers and Are Far More Diverse." Census Bureau QuickFacts. June 25, 2015. https://www.census.gov/newsroom/press-releases/2015/cb15-113.html.

Valencia, Nick. "Shooting Victim's Kin: I Forgive You." CNN, June 20, 2015. YouTube video, 2:35. https://youtu.be/lxa3FmZitlQ.

Vines, Matthew. *God and the Gay Christian: The Biblical Case in Support of Same-Sex Relationships*. New York: Convergent, 2015.

Warnock, Raphael G. *The Divided Mind of the Black Church: Theology, Piety, and Public Witness*. New York University Press, 2014. Accessed February 19, 2019. http://www.jstor.org/stable/j.ctt9qfcsd.

Weems, Lovett H. *Church Leadership: Vision, Team, Culture, and Integrity*. Nashville: Abingdon, 2010.

Wells, Ayla. "Vision And Mission: What Is the Difference?" International Leadership Institute. February 6, 2019. https://iliteam.org/coreleadership/vision-mission.

Bibliography

West, Cornel. "Cornel West: Justice Is What Love Looks Like in Public." Addressed delivered at Howard University. YouTube video, 1:00:00. Uploaded April 17, 2011. https://www.youtube.com/watch?v=nGqP7S_WO6o.

———. "Cornel West: Love and Justice Are Indivisible." Los Angeles Hope Festival, June 14, 2017. *Big Think* video, 9:37. http://bigthink.com/videos/cornel-west-love-and-justice-are-indivisible.

Winder, Terrell J. A. "'Shouting It Out': Religion and the Development of Black Gay Identities." *Qualitative Sociology* 38 (2015) 375–94.

Winograd, Morley, and Michael Hais. "Race? No, Millennials Care Most about Gender Equality." *Atlantic*, October 24, 2013. https://www.theatlantic.com/politics/archive/2013/10/race-no-millennials-care-most-about-gender-equality/430305/.

Winter, Ralph D., and Bruce A. Koch. "Finishing the Task: The Unreached Peoples Challenge." *International Journal of Frontier Missions* 19 (Winter 2002) 15–25. http://www.ijfm.org/PDFs_IJFM/19_4_PDFs/winter_koch_task.pdf

Woodruff, Paul. *Reverence: Renewing a Forgotten Virtue by Paul Woodruff*. New York: Oxford University Press, 2014.

Wyche, Susan P., et al. "Technology in Spiritual Formation." *Proceedings of the 2006 20th Anniversary Conference on Computer Supported Cooperative Work—CSCW '06*, November 11, 2006, 199–208.

www.ingramcontent.com/pod-product-compliance
Lightning Source LLC
Chambersburg PA
CBHW062003180426
43198CB00036B/2173